D1285027

Library and Archives Canada Cataloguing in Publication

McCreesh, Alison, author
Ramshackle : a Yellowknife story / Alison McCreesh.

ISBN 978-1-894994-99-6 (paperback)

1. Yellowknife (N.W.T.)--Social life and customs--Comic books, strips, etc. 2. Yellowknife (N.W.T.)--Description and travel--Comic books, strips, etc. 3. Yellowknife (N.W.T.)--Biography--Comic books, strips, etc. 4. Graphic novels. I. Title.

FC4196.394.M33 2015 971.9'3 C2015-903873-1

First Edition
Printed in Canada by Marquis
BDANG Imprint #16
BDANG logo by Billy Mavreas

Conundrum Press
Greenwich, Nova Scotia, Canada
www.conundrumpress.com

Conundrum Press acknowledges the financial support of the Canada Council for the Arts and the government of Canada through the Canada Book Fund toward its publishing activities.

Canada Council for the Arts Conseil des Arts du Canada

Alison McCreesh would like to thank the NWT Arts Council

Ramshackle

a Yellowknife Story

FOREWORD

When I graduated in the spring of 2009, I started a comic blog aptly – if not very creatively – titled 'Alison a fini l'école,' which loosely translates as 'Alison has finished school'. I was done with being in class and being sedentary and wanted to document my adventures as I hit the road. I'd travelled a fair amount, but past attempts at diaries had always fizzled out after the first week or so. This time, with the world wide web as my witness, I would diligently record my anecdotes. My goal was to post a few comics a week – ideally several, but never less than one. And, surprisingly, I did. I never garnered a vast readership, but a little accountability was all it took. I kept this up for three years, drawing and posting. It didn't matter that I had neither scanner nor laptop. As I travelled, I took photos of pages in my sketchbooks and uploaded them from public libraries or internet cafés.

I suppose one of my secondary motives was somehow turning all this work into a zine or book, but I didn't take that seriously into account while drawing all those little panels. Without a set plan, the comics didn't quite come together in a way that could stand alone. For one, they changed form and style over time. Originally they were single panel gags, which slowly morphed into two-panel strips: sometimes neatly watercoloured, sometimes scribbled onto coffee-stained paper. Moreover, they lacked the context to tie them together. And so, I sat on it all. I moved around, accumulating more sketchbooks (and tattered loose leaf), until I found a way to bring it all together.

Ramshackle is based on these autobiographical comic snapshots from our first summer in Yellowknife. I have redrawn them and retroactively added context, where necessary, but they've remained pretty true to what was most striking to us when we first moved North. Everything is based on true stories, though some anecdotes have been adapted to fit the comic form. The characters are real people and, where I thought those involved would find pleasure in being featured, I kept real names and appearances. The animals featured in the housesitting stories, on the other hand, have mostly been altered and renamed to respect their (and their owners') privacy.

Though the characters are fairly true to life, one thing this book fails to convey is how many are francophone or bilingual. Pat and I speak French together, my job was in French and lots of the people we met and hung out with that summer were French speaking. Seeing how much of the dialogue in *Ramshackle* took place in French, it seems almost odd to have written the book in English. I hesitated, but settled for English, partly because I wanted as many Yellowknifers as possible to read and enjoy it and, mostly, because I couldn't translate 'Honey Bucket' into French. Still though, it bears mentioning how bilingual our summer was; one of the great things about Yellowknife is how diverse and multicultural it is. For such a small, isolated city, a strikingly wide range of ethnicities are represented. But long before people travelled up from the south and mined the land and (eventually) brought their structures and institutions, the Dene called the area home. Today, in Yellowknife, over 20% of the population is aboriginal and, of the 11 official languages recognized in the Northwest Territories, 6 are spoken in a significant number (Dene Suline, Tlicho, South and North Slavey, English and French).

Yellowknife is a mecca of opportunity, but also a place of inequality. Known for having a transient population, it's also a lifelong home for many. It is a party town and a family city. Some people love it, some people hate it. Like anywhere, it can be experienced in many different ways. This book features one snippet of many Yellowknifes: in some ways typical, in some ways unique. It doesn't claim to be a portrait of the town, rather a glimpse through the eyes of two kids in a soccer-mom van.

I hope you enjoy it!

Alison

Ramshackle

a Yellowknife Story

YELLOWKNIFE
JANUARY 2014
CHEERS TO YOU TOO!
CLING
HUH?
?
OH
HA
NO
I WAS JUST TRYING TO THAW MY BEER
HA! HA!
RIGHT.
IT SURE IS COLD
BRRRR
I'M LUKE, BY THE WAY
ALISON
NICE TO MEET YOU, ALISON.
WELL, MEET YOU... NOT THAT I'D EVEN RECOGNIZE YOU WITHOUT ALL YOUR CLOTHES ON.
OOPS!
HA. HA.
THAT'S NOT WHAT I MEANT!

AND THEN, YOU JUST KNOW WHAT'S COMING.
SO, DO YOU LIVE HERE FULL TIME?
HAVE YOU BEEN HERE LONG?
WHAT BROUGHT YOU UP HERE?

TO FINISH MY DEGREE IN FINE ARTS, I HAD TO COMPLETE A TWO-MONTH INTERNSHIP OF MY CHOICE. I DECIDED TO GO TO HALIFAX AND WORK IN AN ARTIST-RUN CENTRE.

IT SEEMED LIKE A COOL CITY, AND I HAD FRIENDS THERE. THEY OFFERED ME A PLACE TO LIVE AND TOOK ME TO PARTIES.

WELL, THAT WAS FUN.

IT'S A SHAME NOBODY ELSE GOT THE MEMO ABOUT IT BEING A "CARNY" THEME.

- FOUR-ARMED GIRL

BEARDED-LADY

NON-DEFINED TRASHY INBRED CHARACTER

ME

YEAH. I HOPE ALL THOSE PEOPLE I WAS MEETING FOR THE FIRST TIME UNDERSTOOD THIS IS A COSTUME. AND THAT MY NAME ISN'T REALLY DARLENE. AND THAT MY PARENTS AREN'T REALLY CLOSELY RELATED.

I FIT RIGHT IN.

THE INTERNSHIP ITSELF WAS ALSO AN INSTRUCTIVE EXPERIENCE.

YOU CALLED MONDAY?

YEAH. SORRY. WE HAD NO PHONE THEN,

BUT WE FINALLY GOT OUR ARTS COUNCIL GRANT, SO NOW IT'S ALL HOOKED BACK UP.

YUP. THE POWER TOO.

I'VE BEEN SORTING CORRESPONDENCE FOR THE LAST HALF HOUR AND EVERY SINGLE LETTER STARTS WITH "SORRY IT'S TAKEN ME THIS LONG TO GET BACK TO YOU."

IT WAS PROBABLY A FAIRLY HONEST REPRESENTATION OF WHAT AWAITED ME IF I CHOSE THIS AS A CAREER PATH.

MY ACTUAL ROLE WAS NEVER CLEARLY DEFINED, BUT THE CAST OF CHARACTERS WAS ENDEARING.
MENU MEEEH- NEEOO MENNNUUU.
OH! JUST USE THE DAMN MOUSE!
I SWEAR! IF YOU GET THE PRONUNCIATION RIGHT, IT WORKS.
MENU MEH-NEW
SHIT!
I FORGOT TO PUT A SKIRT ON!
THIS IS THE SECOND TIME I'VE DONE THIS SINCE CHRISTMAS.
AND I SUPPOSE I DID LEARN A VALUABLE LESSON OR TWO.
GET THE BIRD!
SHOO! SHOO BIRD!
QUICK!
LET'S GET OUT OF HERE!
IF ANOTHER ART STUDENT TELLS ME I HUNG THEIR DRAWING UPSIDE DOWN,
I'M GONNA LOSE IT!
BUT IT'S OUTSIDE...
SHATTERED PLANT POT
Y'KNOW, IF YOUR PIECE IS AN ABSTRACT AND YOU DON'T DO ANY-THING TO INDICATE WHICH SIDE IS UP...
MOSTLY THOUGH, I WAS A SLIGHTLY BAFFLED BYSTANDER.

IT WAS AN UNPAID INTERNSHIP AND I THOUGHT I MIGHT STICK AROUND HALIFAX FOR THE SUMMER. I NEEDED A JOB.

I TRIED TO FIND PART-TIME WORK AND WASN'T TOO PICKY. STILL, IT WAS A TERRIBLE TIME FOR EMPLOYMENT – ESPECIALLY ON THE EAST COAST.

FIRST, I WORKED IN A CALL CENTRE. TROUBLESHOOTING FOR PRESSURE WASHERS AND BBQS.

THIS, HERE, IS THE BBQ.

YOU CAN REFER TO IT WHEN WALKING PEOPLE THROUGH SOLUTIONS.

I LASTED ALL OF TWO DAYS.

THEN I MOVED ON TO VALUE VILLAGE. THERE, I FELT SLIGHTLY MORE QUALIFIED.

SO YOU HANG THE SHIRTS IN ORDER BASED ON THEIR COLOUR.

YELLOW, ORANGE, RED, PINK, ETC.

IT'S TRICKY AT FIRST, BUT YOU'LL FIGURE IT OUT.

MY DEGREE WAS PUT TO USE.

THE INTERNSHIP ENDED AND VALUE VILLAGE BECAME A FULL-TIME GIG. I'D HAVE BEEN FINE WITH IT FOR A WHILE BUT, ONE NIGHT, PAT CALLED WITH A SOMEWHAT BETTER IDEA.
YOU WANT US TO GO WHERE?
AND, WITHIN A WEEK, I HAD LEFT HALIFAX AND MY PROMISING CAREER IN RETAIL BEHIND.

PAT HAD BEEN MY ON-AGAIN, OFF-AGAIN BOYFRIEND FOR THE PAST COUPLE OF YEARS.

WE HAD TAKEN UP AGAIN JUST BEFORE I LEFT FOR THE INTERNSHIP AND HAD MADE PLANS TO REUNITE ONCE WE HAD SETTLED ON A PLACE TO SPEND THE SUMMER.

IN THE MEAN TIME, HE HAD STAYED IN CHICOUTIMI (QC) WHERE WE HAD BOTH BEEN GOING TO SCHOOL.

HAVING PICKED THE NORTHWEST TERRITORIES, I MADE THE TRIP BACK TO CHICOUTIMI. I WAS TO MEET PAT THERE AND THEN WE WOULD HEAD OUT TO YELLOWKNIFE TOGETHER.
I FOUND A RIDE ON KIJIJI. IT SEEMED LIKE THE CHEAPEST WAY TO GET BACK FROM NOVA SCOTIA TO QUEBEC.
OH. I DUNNO.
VISIT ALL THE CONTINENTS, MAYBE.
YOU?
I'D LIKE TO HAVE A MOTOR BIKE.
AND, AT LEAST ONCE, I'D LIKE TO HAVE SEX WITH A SLIM WOMAN.
AS I SAT THROUGH 10 HOURS OF INCREASINGLY UNCOMFORTABLE CONVERSATION. I WISHED I HAD BIT THE BULLET AND PURCHASED A TRAIN TICKET.
Extremely long and awkward ride

REALLY? YOU GUYS WERE JUST LIKE: LET'S GO TO YELLOWKNIFE?
YUP.
BUT, DID YOU KNOW ANYONE HERE?
NOPE
AND YOU DIDN'T HAVE JOBS LINED UP?
NOPE
YOU JUST PACKED YOUR STUFF AND HEADED NORTH?
YUP

MID-MAY 2009 | ON THE ROAD

TO BE FAIR, IT WASN'T THAT BIG OF A DEAL. WE HAD JUST GRADUATED, WE DIDN'T HAVE PROPER JOBS AND PAT'S LEASE WAS UP A FEW WEEKS LATER. THE MASTER PLAN HAD ALWAYS BEEN TO TAKE A YEAR AND GO OFF TRAVELLING. WE HAD JUST THOUGHT WE'D SPEND THE SUMMER WORKING BEFORE WE HIT THE ROAD. ODDS WERE WE'D MAKE MORE MONEY IN THE NORTH THOUGH, SO IT MADE SENSE TO LOOK FOR SUMMER JOBS IN YELLOWKNIFE INSTEAD.

The VAN

ON KIJIJI, WE FOUND WHAT WE WANTED: A SOCCER MOM VAN.

A 1997 PLYMOUTH VOYAGER. $650

THE SELLER: A MOM CALLED LINE.

IN QUEBEC, THE BUYER AND THE SELLER OF A USED VEHICLE HAVE TO GO TOGETHER TO THE LICENSING BUREAU TO SWITCH THE REGISTRATION. IT'S ALWAYS SLIGHTLY AWKWARD. POLITE CONVERSATION IS GENERALLY A BIT STRAINED. WHAT CAN YOU EXPECT? ALL YOU HAVE IN COMMON IS SOME BEATER PARKED OUT FRONT. AND THE NAGGING DOUBT YOU'RE GETTING RIPPED OFF.

TO KILL TIME, I RAMBLED ON.

SO WE'RE GOING TO RIP THE REAR SEATS OUT AND PUT IN A BED. THAT WAY, WE CAN SLEEP IN THE BACK. I MEAN, IT'LL BE A LITTLE CRAMPED, BUT WE'LL SAVE ON CAMPGROUNDS. IT'LL BE SUPER INCONSPICUOUS. WHO SUSPECTS THE SOCCER MOM VAN? AND, WELL, ONCE WE GET THERE, WE CAN CONTIN TO LIVE IN THE VAN. WE' MAKE FRIENDS AND TH LET US PARK IN TH DRIVEWAY. OR SOM I KNEW PEOPL DID THAT

YOU WANT TO GO WHERE?!?

THE KIND LADY GOT A BIT FLUSTERED. SHE DIDN'T WANT ME TO BUY THE VAN ANYMORE – NO WAY WOULD IT MAKE IT 5000 KM ACROSS THE COUNTRY.

I THANKED LINE FOR HER HONESTY
AND, AGAINST MY BETTER JUDGEMENT, BOUGHT IT ANYWAY.
THREE DAYS LATER, THERE WAS A BED IN THE BACK AND WE WERE ON OUR WAY.
I WISH THE TAPE DECK WORKED.
NOPE.
NO RADIO RECEPTION.
THE 'CHECK ENGINE' LIGHT BLINKED OMINOUSLY AND WE WERE HEADED STRAIGHT WEST.

IT WAS A LONG TRIP
5 216 Km
65 hours
DESTINATION
STARTING POINT
NT
NU
AB
SK
MB
BC
ON
USA
Gas Station attendant
NAH. VAL D'OR IS THAT WAY.
SO, TO GET TO VAL D'OR, WE KEEP GOING THIS WAY, RIGHT?
ME→
CHIBOUGAMAU, QC MAY 17th
CHICOUTIMI
QUEBEC CITY
MONTREAL
OTTAWA
TORONTO
QUEBEC
SNOW IN MAY?!
MUMBLE GRUMBLE
STUPID COUNTRY.
USA
ONTARIO
PAT
SOMEWHERE WEST OF HEARST, ON MAY 18th
HA-HA.
YOU LOOK SILLY.
A TUQUE, SOCKS AND NOTHING ELSE
SK
ON
WINNIPEG
IT'S BELOW FREEZING OUT THERE
KEEPING EXTREMITIES WARM IS KEY.
USA
MANITOBA

LANIGAN, SK MAY 19th
A STRIP MALL PARKING LOT?
COULDN'T WE HAVE FOUND ANYWHERE MORE SCENIC TO SPEND THE NIGHT?
THERE'S LIGHT.
AND WE CAN COOK BEHIND THIS DUMPSTER.
IT'LL SHELTER US FROM THIS HORRIBLE WIND.
NWT
ALBERTA
BC
EDMONTON
SASKATCHEWAN
SASKATOON
AB
MB
USA
WE'D BOTH ALREADY CROSSED CANADA BY ROAD ON A HANDFUL OF OCCASIONS SO THE DRIVE AS FAR AS EDMONTON WAS NOTHING EXCITING FOR EITHER OF US.
IS IT FIELD?
IS IT CLOUD?
VEERING STRAIGHT NORTH IN ALBERTA WAS WHERE THE ADVENTURE BEGAN.
FINALLY.
OH. COME ON!
THAT'S NOT HOW "20 QUESTIONS" WORKS!

WE WERE HEADED UP NORTH.

AND SOMETHING ABOUT THE UP AND THE NORTH HAD LED US TO EXPECT SOMETHING STRIKING AND POSTCARD WORTHY:

A CLIMB TO A LAST FRONTIER, ALASKA-HWY STYLE

THERE WERE NO WINDY ROADS THOUGH. NO RAGING RIVERS, NO TURQUOISE LAKES, NO MOUNTAIN SHEEP AND - FOR THAT MATTER - NO MOUNTAINS.

INSTEAD, IT WAS JUST FLAT.

NORTHERN ALBERTA WAS, AT BEST, ANTICLIMACTIC.
AS IT TURNED OUT THOUGH, THE SCENERY WASN'T OUR GREATEST CONCERN.
WHAT IF WE BREAK DOWN 500KM FROM THE NEAREST GARAGE?
NAH.
TOCK! TOCK! TOCK! TOCK!
AS THE TOWNS AND COMMUNITIES GREW FEWER AND FARTHER BETWEEN, THE "CHECK ENGINE" LIGHT SEEMED TO GROW EXPONENTIALLY BRIGHTER AND MORE THREATENING.
Yellowknife
315 Km
Great Slave Lake
Fort Prov.
NWT
141 Km
Enterprise
312 Km
High Level
193 Km
Manning
ALBERTA
Whitecourt
Edmonton
IT'S NOT EVEN WORTH TRYING TO FIX IT.
THE WORK WOULD COST YOU WAY MORE THAN THE VAN IS WORTH.
IT MIGHT HOLD FOR A WHILE,
OR IT MIGHT NOT.
JUST DRIVE IT TILL IT DIES.
THERE WERE ODD SOUNDS AND THE RARE AND SLIGHT INCLINES WERE HARDER TO CLIMB.
SOMETHING WAS DEFINITELY WRONG
WE EVENTUALLY AGREED TO STOP AND HAVE IT CHECKED OUT.
YOU SAID YOU'RE GOING WHERE?!

SO WE DROVE
AND WE PRAYED
WANNA TAKE A PHOTO OR SOMETHING?
MUMBLE GRUMBLE
NORTWEST TERRITORIES 60th parallel
STILL 529 KM BEFORE WE GET TO YELLOWKNIFE.
WE MADE IT TO THE 60th PARALLEL
WHERE'S THE DOCK?
WE MUST BE IN THE WRONG PLACE.
WE'RE GOOD.
IT'LL JUST SLAM INTO THE SHORE.
THEY DO THAT IN THE YUKON TOO.
316 KM TO GO.
WE MADE IT TO THE MACKENZIE RIVER.
AND WE DROVE
ATTENTION
NEXT 210 km
WHAT?!
WILD BISON?!
WE DON'T HAVE BISON IN THE WILD IN CANADA...
DO WE?
WE MADE IT ACROSS THE MACKENZIE
AND WE WILLED THE VAN FORWARD.
OH MY GOD!
LOOK AT THE BABIES.
SLOW DOWN.
I WANT TO TAKE A PHOTO.
NO.
NO DON'T STOP!
THAT BIG ONE'S GIVING US THE EVIL EYE.
WE MADE IT PAST LOTS OF BISON.

AND, AGAINST ALL ODDS, WE MADE IT TO YELLOWKNIFE
OH.
THEY HAVE BIG BUILDINGS.

WOW. SO THE VAN MADE IT.
$650 WELL SPENT
HOW LONG DID IT TAKE ALTOGETHER?

A WEEK FROM CHICOUTIMI TO YELLOWKNIFE.
WELL, MAYBE 6.5 DAYS.

YOU GUYS MUST HAVE BEEN SO HAPPY AND EXCITED WHEN YOU GOT HERE!
YEAH YOU'D HAVE THOUGHT...

LET'S TURN AROUND AGAIN.
NOW MY BUM'S WARM BUT MY NOSE IS FROZEN.

YELLOWKNIFE
SUMMER 2009

WE DROVE INTO TOWN AND PULLED INTO THE FIRST PARKING LOT WE SAW.

WE WANTED OUT OF THE VAN. **IMMEDIATELY.**

FIRST IMPRESSIONS

MY PRIOR EXPERIENCE OF THE NORTH HAD BEEN THE YUKON.

HAD I SOMEHOW IMAGINED THAT YELLOWKNIFE WOULD ALSO HAVE THAT QUAINT GOLDRUSH LOOK?

I GUESS I HAD.

WE WANDERED AROUND A LITTLE
HUH
YK CENTRE
WE WERE TRYING TO GET OUR BEARINGS,
TRYING TO GET A FEEL FOR IT.
THIS WAY?
SURE
WE SHOULD HAVE BEEN EXCITED TO HAVE FINALLY MADE IT,
OR FAILING THAT, AT LEAST EXCITED THAT THE VAN HAD MADE IT.
I SUPPOSE WE SHOULD TRY AND TRACK DOWN OUR HOSTS...
Centre Square Parkade
YEAH, I GUESS.
INSTEAD, WE JUST FELT EMPTY.

BEFORE HITTING THE ROAD, WE HAD CONTACTED SOME PEOPLE IN YELLOWKNIFE. THEY SAID WE COULD PARK IN THEIR DRIVEWAY FOR THE FIRST FEW DAYS – TO CALL THEM ONCE WE GOT TO TOWN.

A PAY PHONE?!
GOOD LUCK WITH THAT.
REDDI MART
THEY'VE BEEN SO BADLY VANDALIZED THAT THEY HAD TO TAKE THEM ALL OUT.
IN HINDSIGHT, I WOULD SURMISE THAT THE ABSENCE OF PAYPHONES WAS MORE LIKELY DUE TO THE CHANGING OF THE TIMES, BUT AT THAT MOMENT IT WAS SIMPLY ANOTHER BLACK MARK AGAINST YELLOWKNIFE.
THE TOWN WAS UGLY AND THE PEOPLE WERE NASTY PHONE WRECKERS.
I SUPPOSE WE SHOULD DRIVE OUT OF TOWN AND FIND A PLACE TO PARK FOR THE NIGHT.
...

I INSISTED WE DRIVE AROUND A LITTLE MORE. WITH A BIT OF LUCK, WE MIGHT YET FIND A PAY PHONE.

WE SHOULD HAVE ASKED THOSE GUYS FOR THEIR ADDRESS AS WELL AS THEIR PHONE NUMBER.

I DON'T WANT TO SLEEP IN A PARKING LOT.
I WOULDN'T FEEL SAFE.

I MEAN, IF WHAT THESE PEOPLE HAVE DONE TO THEIR PAY PHONES IS ANYTHING TO GO BY...

IT WAS LATE, WE WERE TIRED AND WHATEVER ADRENALINE HAD BEEN KEEPING US GOING FOR THE PAST FEW DAYS HAD RUN OUT.

IT WON'T BE THAT BAD.
WE'LL MAKE FRIENDS AND EVERYTHING WILL BE OKAY.

THAT NIGHT, WE NEVER DID FIND A PAYPHONE
WE DROVE TO WHAT WE MISTAKENLY THOUGHT TO BE THE EDGE OF TOWN AND HUNKERED DOWN NEXT TO SOME BIG RECYCLING BINS.
PAAAAAT?
WE HAD A PLACE FOR THE NIGHT.
MMMM?
IT'S NOT GOING TO GET MUCH DARKER IS IT?
I DOUBT IT.
MINI GOLF
PAAAAAT?
MMMMM?
IF YOU REALLY DON'T LIKE IT HERE, WE DON'T HAVE TO STAY FOR THE ENTIRE SUMMER
SHHHHHHH.

THE DEAL WITH YELLOWKNIFE
62°26'3"N 114°23'51"W
400 KM SOUTH OF THE ARCTIC CIRCLE
SOME NUMBERS
POPULATION: Approx 20,000
ABORIGINAL: Approx 22%
AVERAGE AGE: 32.3 (Canada-wide average 39.5)
AVERAGE FAMILY INCOME: $124,200 (with 10% of families earning less than $30,000)
MOTHER TONGUE
• ENGLISH ▸ 82%
• ABORIGINAL LANGUAGE (Inuktitut, Tlicho, North Slavey, South Slavey) ▸ 4%
• FRENCH ▸ 4%
• TAGALOG ▸ 2.3%
• VIETNAMESE
• CHINESE
ARCTIC OCEAN
INUVIK Pop: 3,400
YT
NWT
NU
FORT SIMPSON Pop: 1,245
Pop: 20,000 YELLOWKNIFE
B.C.
HAY RIVER Pop: 3,700
AB
FORT SMITH Pop: 2,500
SK
TOTAL NWT POP: 43,600
A BRIEF HISTORY OF YELLOWKNIFE
SINCE TIME IMMEMORIAL
SLAVEY, TLICHO AND CHIPEWYAN-SPEAKING DENE INHABIT THE AREA.
THEY DO NOT SPECIFICALLY LIVE IN THE AREA THAT WILL BECOME YELLOWKNIFE, BUT BY THE 1930s, THEY HAVE A SETTLEMENT NEARBY: DETTAH.
THE WHITE MAN CALLS THE NEW SETTLEMENT "YELLOWKNIFE" BECAUSE OF THE COPPER BLADED TOOLS USED BY THE DENE.
THE DENE CALL YELLOWKNIFE SOMBAK'E: "MONEY PLACE"
FUR TRADE
NEW FOLKS ARRIVE IN THE AREA:
- METIS FAMILIES AND
- FUR TRADE COMPANY EXPLORERS
1700s
YELLOWKNIFE IS A FUEL CACHE FOR AERIAL EXPLORATION OF THE ARCTIC
1920s
TURNS OUT THERE IS GOLD
GOLD
1933-1939 STAKING OF MINES CLAIMS
KLONDIKE?
WHILE THE GOLDRUSH WAS IN FULL SWING FURTHER WEST IN THE YUKON FROM 1896 TO 1899, THE NWT WAS DISMISSED AS BEING FAR AWAY AND TOO HARD TO ACCESS

OPULATION INCREASES to 1000.
WILDCAT CAFE
WEAVER & DEVORE
CANADIAN BANK OF COMMERCE
ORONA INN
SETTLEMENT BOOMING
1936
1937
1938
1939
1942
5 GOLD MINES in PRODUCTION in the region.
1943 LULL FOR WAR EFFORTS
1944
MASSIVE POST-WAR STAKING RUSH
1945-1946-1947
ORIGINAL SETTLEMENT TOO CROWDED
NEW TOWNSITE IS ESTABLISHED
MORE GROWTH
YELLOWKNIFE BECOMES A MUNICIPALITY
1953
1951 POP: 2,724
1961 POP: 3,245
MORE GOLD
1960 YELLOWKNIFE HWY BUILT
GROWTH - GROWTH - GROWTH
1967
YELLOWKNIFE OFFICIALLY BECOMES THE CAPITAL OF THE NWT
INFLUX OF GOVERNMENT WORKERS
WORK-PROSPERITY
MINING-GOVERNMENT WORK-
1971 POP: 6,122
1981 POP: 9,483
DIAMOND MINES
1991 POP: 17,275
MINES CLOSE, DOWNSIZING OF GOVERNMENT WORK FORCE
1990-1999
ON ANOTHER NOTE: THE DEAL WITH THE RECYCLING BINS
YELLOWKNIFE DOESN'T DO DOOR-TO-DOOR RECYCLING COLLECTION.
INSTEAD THERE ARE BLUE BIN RECYCLING STATIONS FOR PEOPLE TO DROP OFF THEIR OWN RECYCLING
Donald's
2001 POP: 17,772
1999
2003
2004
2005
2007
2009 POP: 19,874
TODAY
MAJOR EMPLOYERS: (in no particular order)
- DIAMOND MINES
- GOVERNMENT OF CANADA
- CITY OF YELLOWKNIFE
- GOVERNMENT OF THE NWT
- TRANSPORTATION
- TOURISM
- ETC.

Mac's

DAY ONE
OLD TOWN
ON OUR VERY FIRST MORNING IN YELLOWKNIFE, WE WOKE UP COLD, STIFF AND MISERABLE. MIRACULOUSLY, WE LOCATED A PHONE AND CONTACTED MYLÈNE AND RUDY, THE COUCH-SURFING HOSTS.
THEY HAD TO WORK, BUT GAVE US DIRECTIONS TO THEIR PLACE. A LADY CALLED DIANE WOULD MEET US THERE AT 10:30, THEY SAID.
THEY LIVED IN OLD TOWN - A NEIGHBOURHOOD WE MISSED WHEN DRIVING AROUND THE NIGHT BEFORE.
SO, WE JUST HANG OUT THERE 'TIL THAT LADY SHOWS UP?
Mylène & Rudy's Building
I SUPPOSE SO.
THIS 'OLD TOWN' SEEMED A LOT MORE APPEALING ALREADY
FROM THAT DRIVEWAY ALONE, WE COULD SEE ALL KINDS OF COOL THINGS:
1 FUNKY ARCHITECTURE
2 A DINOSAUR HOUSE
3 A RAVEN'S NEST IN A CRANE

IT WAS VERY KIND OF OUR HOSTS TO HAVE SET US UP WITH A LOCAL CONNECTION.
SO, ARE YOU READY?
TRUE NORTHERN HOSPITALITY, WE SUPPOSED.
LET'S WALK. I CAN SHOW YOU SOME SIGHTS ALONG THE WAY.
STILL, WE WERE A LITTLE CONFUSED.
PARTICULARLY BY THE NOTION THAT SHE WAS TO 'TAKE US TO SHOWER.'
FIRST, WE CAN STOP AT THE DOCK AND SEE HOW THE ICE IS DOING.
JUST ACROSS THE STREET HERE.
BREAK-UP IS LATE THIS YEAR.
YOU TWO SHOULD RIDE YOUR BIKES OUT ONTO THE LAKE.
GO AS FAR AS YOU CAN.
TAKE A PICNIC.
THIS IS LIKELY ONE OF THE LAST DAYS IT'S SOLID ENOUGH TO RIDE ON.
...
BUT THERE'S OPEN WATER ON THE EDGE.
HOUSE-BOATS

THIS WAS MORE LIKE IT. MORE WHAT WE HAD HOPED FOR. MORE DIFFERENT.
HOW DO PEOPLE GET TO THEIR HOUSES?
IN THE SUMMER, THEY PADDLE MOSTLY
SOME HAVE MOTORBOATS.
IN THE WINTER THEY WALK OR DRIVE.
IN BETWEEN SEASONS IS TRICKY.
SOON, PEOPLE'LL BE HAVING TO DRAG THEIR CANOES BESIDE THEM TO BE SAFE.
DIANE TOLD US ABOUT THE HOUSEBOATS. HOW THERE WERE ABOUT 20 OF THEM IN YELLOWKNIFE BAY. HOW PEOPLE LIVED THERE YEAR-ROUND. HOW IT WAS IMPORTANT TO MAKE SURE YOUR HOUSEBOAT FROZE IN LEVEL AT THE START OF WINTER.
I HAD SO MANY QUESTIONS
BUT THERE WAS THE BUSINESS OF SHOWERING TO ATTEND TO.
IT'S NOT FAR
AND THERE'S A NICE BIG BATHROOM YOU'LL SEE.
MYLÈNE AND RUDY HAVE A SMALL WATER TANK
AND WITH THEM ALREADY HAVING A HOUSE GUEST...
NEXT WATER DELIVERY IS FRIDAY.
THAT'S A FEW DAYS OFF YET.
IT WOULD BE A PAIN FOR THEM TO RUN OUT OF WATER.
ANYWAY, WHERE I'M HOUSESITTING I'VE BARELY USED THE WATER.
THEY'LL BE SWITCHING TO SURFACE LINES FOR THE SUMMER SOON, THEN WE WON'T HAVE TO WORRY ANYMORE.

AND SO WE BATHED PROPERLY FOR THE FIRST TIME IN A WEEK AND DIANE FED US BRUNCH.
YELLOWKNIFE SEEMED MUCH BETTER ALREADY.
WHAT A NICE HOUSE.
YOU LIVE HERE?
NO, NO.
AS I SAID EARLIER, I'M JUST HOUSESITTING.
I'M AN ARTIST AND I CAN'T AFFORD TO PAY RENT IN THIS TOWN.
PRICES ARE OUTRAGEOUS.
I'M BARELY EVER WITHOUT A PLACE TO LIVE.
WITH YELLOWKNIFE BEING SO ISOLATED, WHEN PEOPLE GET TIME OFF WORK, THEY HEAD OUT.
OFTEN FOR WEEKS AT A TIME.
PEOPLE HAVE PETS AND PLANTS,
AND THEY DON'T LIKE TO LEAVE THEIR HOUSES EMPTY.
ESPECIALLY DURING THE WINTER.
I'VE BEEN DOING THIS FOR YEARS.
MOVING ALL THE TIME GETS A BIT ANNOYING.
BUT IT'S A SMALL PRICE TO PAY.
RAF
RAF
RAF
RAF
RAF
RAF
AND HAVING TO DEAL WITH OTHER PEOPLE'S PETS...
RAF
RAF
RAF
RAF
...WELL.
RAF RAF RAF
RAF
ARE YOU GUYS READY FOR OUR TOUR?

DIANE TOOK US ON A WALKING TOUR OF OLD TOWN. IT WAS A FASCINATING PLACE. AN ECLECTIC COMBINATION OF NEW AND OLD. OF HIGH END AND RAMSHACKLE.
I HAD EYES ONLY FOR THE CROOKED LITTLE HOUSES.
IT'S SO FUNNY TO SEE LITTLE CABINS HIDING BEHIND BIG EXPENSIVE HOUSES.
DO PEOPLE LIVE IN THEM?
OR ARE THEY JUST FUNKY SHEDS?
SOME ARE INHABITED, NOT ALL OF THEM THOUGH.
THERE USED TO BE WAY MORE.
UP UNTIL THE EARLY 80S, THIS WHOLE AREA WAS ALMOST EXCLUSIVELY SHACKS.
IT WAS CHAOS,
BUT IT WAS A GREAT TIME.

IN THE MID-80s, THE CITY BECAME REALLY AGRES-SIVE ABOUT TRYING TO GENTRIFY OLD TOWN. THEY WERE INTENT ON CRACKING DOWN ON SQUATTING.
THEY EVEN CAME UP WITH SOMETHING THEY CALLED THE "SQUATTER POLICY."
IT'S AROUND THAT TIME THAT PEOPLE STARTED BUILDING HOUSEBOATS.
MOVED OUT OF THE CITY'S JURISDICTION.
PEOPLE GOT ORGANIZED AND FOUGHT BACK.
THANK GOD.
STILL THOUGH.

OLD TOWN'S ONLY A SHADOW OF ITS FORMER SELF.
THE CITY HAS BECOME MORE ACCEPTING OVER TIME, BUT IT STILL ISN'T GREAT.
THINGS ARE CHANGING FAST DOWN HERE. OLD BUILDINGS GET TORN DOWN, NEW CONSTRUCTION GOES UP.

THE DEAL WITH TRUCKED WATER

YELLOWKNIFE HAS LONG SINCE GROWN FROM A FRONTIER SETTLEMENT TO A MODERN CAPITAL CITY.
BUT PEOPLE STILL LIVE IN OLD TOWN, AND OLD TOWN REMAINS BUILT ON ROCK- AND CONTINUES TO WRESTLE WITH PERMAFROST.
SO NOW, IN OLD TOWN, THERE ARE
INDOOR
TANKS
UNDER-GROUND (with much effort)
WATER
AND THERE ARE
TRUCKS
SEWAGE
"NECTAR OF THE GODS"
AND YOU THINK YOUR JOB SUCKS!
YUP. THAT'S REALLY WHAT IT SAYS ON THE TRUCKS.
THE TRUCKS COME ON SCHEDULE, TWICE A WEEK: THEY DELIVER WATER, AND THEY PUMP OUT SEWAGE.
IT'S A PRETTY GOOD SYSTEM, UNLESS
YOU RUN OUT OF WATER
a) BECAUSE OF PARTIES.
We're on trucked water! IF IT'S YELLOW, LET IT MELLOW. IF IT'S BROWN, FLUSH IT DOWN. thanks! :)
b) BECAUSE OF LANDLORDS WHO HAVE TOO MANY APARTMENTS/ROOMMATES SHARING ONE TANK.
OR
YOU HAVE PUMPOUT ISSUES:
(i.e. you don't get pumped out)
a) BECAUSE YOU HAVE SOMETHING BLOCKING YOUR PUMPOUT.
NO PARK
PUMPOUT
WED AM
b) BECAUSE YOUR PIPES FREEZE (Generally from underuse)
Infamous "Could not pump out" slip hanging on doorknob

IN THE SUMMERTIME, ONCE IT DOESN'T FREEZE ANYMORE, THERE ARE SURFACE LINES. AT THE BEGINNING OF JUNE, THE CITY TURNS THE WATER ON AND THEN IT'S JUST LIKE ANYWHERE ELSE FOR THREE MONTHS...
EW. IT'S GROSS IN HERE. YOU SHOULD COME AND CHECK IT OUT.
...UNTIL EARLY SEPTEMBER, WHEN EVERYONE RUSHES TO CLEAN OUT THEIR WATER TANK BEFORE A NEW SEASON BEGINS.
FYI
TRUCKED WATER ISN'T SPECIFIC TO YELLOWKNIFE'S OLD TOWN. OTHER ROCKIER PARTS OF THE CITY HAVE IT TOO. AS DO MOST COMMUNITIES IN THE ARCTIC WHERE PERMAFROST IS AN ISSUE.
WAIT!
WAIT!
DELIVERY IS KNOWN TO BE LESS RELIABLE IN SMALL COMMUNITIES: DESPERATELY CHASING DOWN THE WATER TRUCK IS NOT UNCOMMON.
ALSO, IT'S INTERESTING TO NOTE THAT IN THE TOWN OF INUVIK, THEY HAVE AN ALTERNATIVE: THE UTILIDOR
ARCTIC OCEAN
ARCTIC CIRCLE
YT
NWT
NU
BC
AB
SK
MB
ON
AN INSULATED ABOVE-GROUND SYSTEM THAT WINDS THROUGH THE TOWN (AND COMPLICATES SHORTCUTS).

SETTLING IN
WE HAD COME TO YELLOWKNIFE TO FIND WORK AND WERE INTENT ON FINDING JOBS QUICKLY.
ANY IDEAS AS TO WHAT YOU'D LIKE TO DO FOR WORK?
I'D BE OPEN TO ANYTHING REALLY.
JUST NOT OFFICE WORK.
SOMETHING OUTSIDE, I THINK.
HOUSE PAINTING MAYBE?
JUST NOT LANDSCAPING AGAIN.
THIS WOULD BE A GREAT OPPORTUNITY TO TRY SOMETHING NEW.
BUT SOMEHOW, OUR JOB HUNTING WENT AWRY.
YOU HAVE EXPERIENCE WITH CUSTOMER SERVICE?
YOU KNOW HOW TO USE MICROSOFT OFFICE?
YOU'RE BILINGUAL?
YOU KNOW HOW TO DO RESEARCH AND WRITE A REPORT?
YOU KNOW ANYTHING ABOUT TOURISM?
YOU EVER PRUNE TREES?
YOU CAN BACK A TRAILER UP?
YOU HAVE EXPERIENCE LANDSCAPING?
YOU KNOW HOW TO DO BRICKWORK?
YOU CAN DRIVE A BOBCAT?
WITHIN 48 HOURS, WE WERE EMPLOYED. PAT LANDSCAPING, ME IN AN OFFICE.

LIVING ARRANGEMENTS

HAVING MYLÈNE AND RUDY'S DRIVEWAY WAS HELPFUL, BUT BY NO MEANS WAS IT AN IDEAL OR PERMANENT SOLUTION.

FOR ONE, BECAUSE OF THE LAYOUT OF THEIR APARTMENT, WE COULD NEVER TELL IF THEY WERE UP OR ASLEEP.

DO YOU THINK THEY'RE AWAKE YET?
DUNNO
AAARG.

YOU COULD PEE BEHIND SOME BUSHES.
WHAT BUSHES?!

MOREOVER, WE HAD TO GET UP AT 6 AM ON TUESDAY AND FRIDAY MORNINGS.
BEEP BEEP BEEP
WAKE UP!
THE ALARM'S GOING OFF.
MMUMBLE GRMMMBLE
WE HAVE TO MOVE THE VAN.
WE WANTED TO BE SURE WE WEREN'T BLOCKING ACCESS FOR THE WATER OR THE SEWAGE TRUCKS.

THERE WAS ALSO THE ISSUE OF THE OTHER TENANTS WHOSE DRIVEWAY THIS ALSO WAS...
SPIT!
...TO SAY NOTHING OF THE SLIGHTLY PERPLEXED NEIGHBOURS.

WE HAD TO FIND SOMEWHERE ELSE TO PARK.

RENT IS EXPENSIVE IN YELLOWKNIFE AND WE WERE ONLY THERE FOR THE SUMMER, WE WERE DETERMINED TO LIVE IN OUR VAN.

THAT VACANT LOT HAD MANY ADVANTAGES.
WE HAD A PICNIC TABLE TO EAT AND COOK ON,
AH-HA!
IT'S FINALLY LIT!
Acting as human shield
WE JUST NEED TO KEEP IT SHELTERED FROM THE WIND.
Coleman
BUT I'M COLD WITH MY HOODIE UNZIPPED
AND THIS IS REALLY UN-COMFORTABLE.
Coleman
IT'LL ONLY BE 10 MINUTES...
...ONCE THE WATER REACHES A BOIL.
AS WELL AS ACCESS TO WATER TO CLEAN UP AFTER.
COME ON!
frigid barely thawed lake
LET'S GET THE DISHES OVER WITH.
?
ROAD CLOSED

WE WERE WORKING A LOT, DIDN'T YET HAVE A SOCIAL CIRCLE AND WERE INTENT ON NOT SPENDING MONEY.
AS A RESULT, WE SPENT A LOT OF TIME TOGETHER AND TRIED TO MAKE CREATIVE USE OF OUR SURROUNDINGS.
OKAY.
ALL CLEAR
communal recycling bins
THERE'S A BIG STACK OF OLD 'PEOPLE' MAGAZINES
I CAN'T QUITE REACH.
GNA
GNA
PLASTIC
trashy outdated magazines
PAT SPENT ALL DAY WORKING OUTSIDE AND, BY THE EVENING, JUST WANTED TO RELAX. HE HAD LITTLE PATIENCE FOR MY GAMES.
MY INGENUITY WAS LOST ON HIM.
COME AND PUSH
PLEEEAASE
hazardous playground aparatus
CREAK
CREAK
CREAK
IT'S REALLY STIFF
YOU'RE GOING TO GET TETANUS OFF THAT THING.
CREAK
CREAK
CREAK
CREAK
IF WE PICK UP ENOUGH SPEED THE MOSQUITOS WON'T BE ABLE TO KEEP UP.

THE WEATHER WARMED UP AND THE MOSQUITOS GOT WORSE AND WORSE.
BECAUSE OF THIS, WE SPENT MORE AND MORE TIME IN THE VAN.
EW. THESE ARE DAMP.
IT SMELLS OF WET DOG IN HERE.
WHERE ELSE AM I SUPPOSED TO HANG MY WORK CLOTHES?
THIS WAS NEITHER FUN NOR ROMANTIC,
NOR DID IT FULLY SOLVE THE MOSQUITO PROBLEM.
AH-HA
GOT HIM!
SQUISH
ONE MORE CORPSE FOR MY COLLECTION.
THE CEILING IS DISGUSTING
WE HAVE TO CLEAN IT.
NO.
LET IT BE A WARNING TO THE OTHERS.
AND I LIKE COUNTING THEM TO PUT MYSELF TO SLEEP.

WE DID OUR BEST TO MAKE THE VAN A MOSQUITO-FREE ZONE,
THIS SHOULD DO IT...
Duct tape
HA!
THERE'S A VENT WE MISSED DOWN HERE
PASS ME THE TAPE!
HEY, PAT?
WHAT IF WE'VE SEALED THE VAN SO WELL THAT WE SUFFOCATE?
PAAAAT
PLEASE
IT'S 5 AM.
JUST IGNORE IT.
SLAP!
SLAP!
BANG!
YOU BASTARD!
SLAP!
BANG
BUT THIS WAS A BATTLE WE SIMPLY COULD NOT WIN.

OH MY GOD!
HOW CAN THEY POSSIBLY FLY THIS FAST?!
YK CENTRE

MULTI-PURPOSE NALGENE

HAVE FUN SITTING AT YOUR DESK!
HAVE FUN SHOVELLING DIRT ALL DAY!

THE OFFICE JOB
MAKING USE OF OFFICE WASHROOM (TOO LITERALLY)
I HAD JUST FINISHED SCHOOL AND THE LAST THING I WANTED WAS TO SPEND 8 HOURS A DAY IN FRONT OF A COMPUTER SCREEN.
I HAD WANTED SOMETHING OUTSIDE.
SOMETHING GRUBBY AND PHYSICAL.
SOMETHING CLEAR AND TANGIBLE.
MORNING!
DOING SELF-MOTIVATED RESEARCH ON TOURISM DEVELOPMENT WAS THE EXACT OPPOSITE.

SITTING AT A DESK ALL DAY, WATCHING THE CLOCK.

UNDER THE GLARE OF THE FLUORESCENT LIGHTS. TRYING TO FOCUS AND BE PRODUCTIVE.

SCRATCH SCRATCH

I'M GOING OVER TO THE POST OFFICE TO GET THE MAIL.

FINDING EXCUSES TO GET UP AND MOVE AROUND.

BATTLING THE TEMPTATIONS OF THE INTERNET.

ANYBODY WANT ANYTHING FROM SHOPPERS DRUGMART?

STRUGGLING NOT TO RELENTLESSLY CHECK FACEBOOK.

STRUGGLING NOT TO SPEND TIME READING OTHER PEOPLE'S COMIC BLOGS.

MUNCH MUNCH MUNCH MUNCH MUNCH MUNCH

YOU OKAY?

UGH. A LITTLE QUEEZY.

TOO MANY YOGHURT COVERED RAISINS FROM SHOPPERS.

STRUGGLING NOT TO REFRESH MY PERSONAL EMAIL EVERY TWO MINUTES.

AREN'T YOU THE HARD WORKER!

DON'T STAY TOO LATE!

ALL THESE STRUGGLES, I LOST PITIFULLY.

DESPITE MY BEST EFFORTS TO THE CONTRARY, I WOULD SPEND HOURS - GUILT RIDDEN - PROCRASTINATING ONLINE.

IN THE EVENINGS, I WOULD STAY LATER, TRYING TO MAKE UP FOR ALL THAT WASTED TIME.

LUCKY FOR ME, AS OTHER PEOPLE TOOK THEIR SUMMER HOLIDAYS, I HAD RESPONSIBILITIES ADDED TO MY LIST:
MANAGING INCOMING TOURISM INQUIRIES WAS A FAVOURITE OF MINE.
YES
YES
WE DO HAVE A GROCERY STORE.
NOPE
WE'RE NORTH OF ALBERTA
UH-HUH
I'M PRETTY SURE YOU'RE CONFUSING US WITH NEWFOUNDLAND.
HUM.
WELL, THEY'RE NOT "OUR INDIANS,"
AND NO, WE DON'T « HAVE PROBLEMS WITH THEM."
UH-HUH
UH-HUH
NO
THAT'S THE YUKON
YES.
WE DO HAVE A HOSPITAL
EXCUSE-ME?
MY ACCENT?
NO
I SWEAR I'M NOT TURKISH
YES
WE HAVE ROADS
AND BUILDINGS
AND RUNNING WATER
NO
NO
NO POLAR BEARS IN YELLOWKNIFE
YOU'LL BE FINE
CAN-CAN DANCERS?
PANNING FOR GOLD?
NO, THAT'S NOT US
THAT'S THE YUKON.

ACTING AS A RECEPTIONIST WASN'T TOO OBJECTIONABLE EITHER.
YES, HOW CAN I HELP YOU?
SOMEONE FROM YOUR OFFICE JUST LEFT ME A VOICEMAIL
I'M RETURNING HIS CALL
I THINK IT WAS YOUR AFRICAN
CAN YOU TRANSFER ME, PLEASE?
ON THE OTHER HAND, I FOUND HELPING JOBSEEKERS SOMEWHAT DRAINING.
I TAUGHT PRIMARY SCHOOL FOR 30 YEARS
OKAY...
ANY VOLUNTEERING?
I WAS A MARRIAGE COUNSELOR FOR MY CHURCH,
AND I WAS IN THE CHOIR
UH-HUH
I'M NOT SURE HOW WE CAN SPIN THIS ON YOUR RESUMÉ.
YOU'RE SURE YOU WANT TO BE A PREP COOK?
SO,
WHAT KIND OF EMPLOYMENT ARE YOU LOOKING FOR?
WHATEVER
I DON'T CARE.
OOO-KAY...
REALLY, NO SPECIFIC INTERESTS OR SKILLS?
I JUST MOVED HERE,
TO BE ELIGIBLE FOR WELLFARE, I NEED TO WORK A BIT.

GENERALLY, AS LONG AS I WASN'T STARING AT A SCREEN, I COULD FIND ENTERTAINMENT VALUE IN MOST THINGS.

LISTEN TO THIS ONE:

WHAT A **LONG** TITLE!

« REGIONAL DIRECTOR, CLIENT SERVICE TEAM: ALBERTA/NWT PUBLIC WORKS AND GOVERNMENT SERVICES CANADA »

I BET YOU CAN'T BEAT THAT!

OH YEAH?

EARLIER, I GOT: « MANAGER, ECOSYSTEM INITIATIVE, STRATEGIC INTEGRATION AND PARTNERSHIP DIVISION, PRAIRIES AND NORTHERN REGION, ENVIRONMENT CANADA »

OKAY.

YOU WIN THIS ROUND.

GOOD THING WE'RE USING 9x12 ENVELOPES.

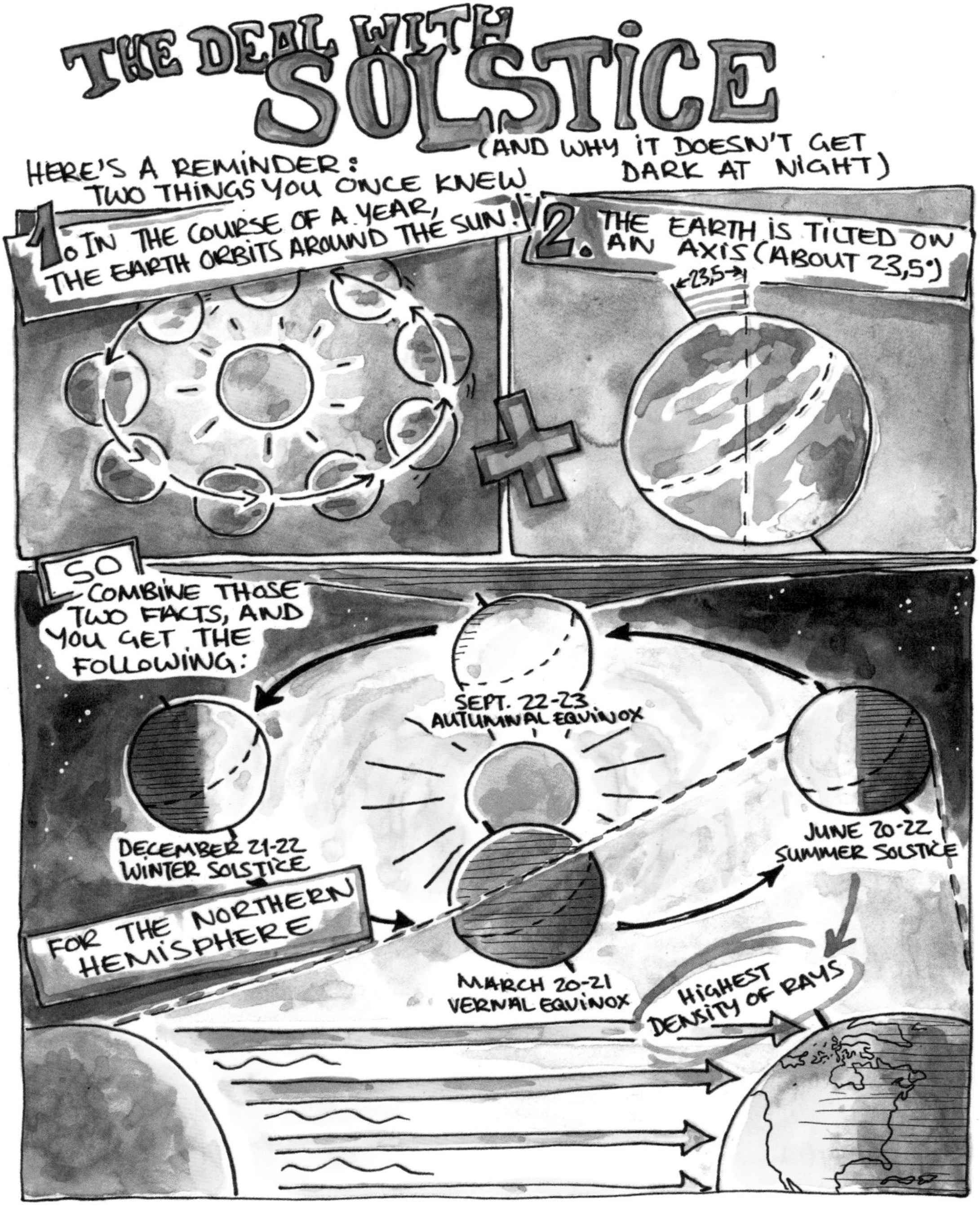

THE DEAL WITH SOLSTICE

(AND WHY IT DOESN'T GET DARK AT NIGHT)

HERE'S A REMINDER:
TWO THINGS YOU ONCE KNEW

1. IN THE COURSE OF A YEAR, THE EARTH ORBITS AROUND THE SUN!

2. THE EARTH IS TILTED ON AN AXIS (ABOUT 23,5°)

23,5

SO COMBINE THOSE TWO FACTS, AND YOU GET THE FOLLOWING:

SEPT. 22-23
AUTUMNAL EQUINOX

DECEMBER 21-22
WINTER SOLSTICE

JUNE 20-22
SUMMER SOLSTICE

FOR THE NORTHERN HEMISPHERE

MARCH 20-21
VERNAL EQUINOX

HIGHEST DENSITY OF RAYS

ON SUMMER SOLSTICE
NORTH POLE
TILTED TOWARDS THE SUN.
THE FURTHER NORTH YOU GO, THE MORE DAYLIGHT HOURS YOU GET.
ARCTIC CIRCLE
EQUATOR
RELATED TRIVIA!
UNTIL SOLSTICE, DAYS GET LONGER. AFTER SOLSTICE, DAYS GET SHORTER.
A few days before and after, the sun seems to stand still in the sky... THUS, THE NAME SOLSTICE
In latin: SOL = SUN
STISTERE = STAND STILL
NORTH OF THE ARCTIC CIRCLE, THE SUN DOESN'T SET AT ALL. THEY GET MIDNIGHT SUN.
(It's not rare to see kids out riding their bikes around in the middle of the night)
ABORIGINAL DAY
TRADITIONALLY SUMMER SOLSTICE IS MARKED IN ONE WAY OR ANOTHER AROUND THE WORLD.
BECAUSE OF ITS CULTURAL RELEVANCE, JUNE 21ST HAS OFFICIALLY BEEN DESIGNATED 'ABORIGINAL DAY' IN CANADA SINCE 1996.
IN THE NWT, WHERE THERE IS SUCH A LARGE ABORIGINAL POPULATION, JUNE 21ST IS A STAT HOLIDAY AND THE DAY IS WIDELY CELEBRATED.
YELLOWKNIFE, HOWEVER, IS SOUTH OF THE ARCTIC CIRCLE. THERE IS NO MIDNIGHT SUN, BUT THERE IS MIDNIGHT TWILIGHT.
24h
20h
16h
12h
8h
4h
0h
NIGHT
NIGHT
DAY
JAN FEB MAR APR MAY JUN JUL AUG SEPT. OCT. NOV. DEC
DAILY HOURS OF DAYLIGHT AND TWILIGHT – Yellowknife, NT

DON'T FORGET TO BUY PROPANE ON YOUR LUNCH BREAK.
WE CAN'T KEEP EATING PB&J SANDWICHES FOR THREE MEALS A DAY.

CABIN FEVER
I THOUGHT IT NEVER RAINED HERE?
THAT THIS WAS A NORTHERN DESERT.
WE WERE GETTING GRUMPY.
IT DOESN'T RAIN MUCH,
WE JUST NOTICE IT MORE.
JUST GO TO SLEEP.
OR PLAY YOUR GUITAR.
OR HERE, HAVE A MAGAZINE.
TOO BRIGHT TO SLEEP.
WE WERE SPENDING TOO MUCH TIME TOGETHER.
Mmumble Grumble
WE NEEDED TO GET OUT MORE,
HUH?
LISTEN TO THIS: TOM CRUISE IS FINALLY GETTING A DIVORCE...
WE NEEDED TO MEET PEOPLE.
...FROM NICOLE KIDMAN?!
HEY.
HOW OLD IS THIS STUPID MAGAZINE?!

MAKING FRIENDS
YELLOWKNIFE IS A TRANSIENT CITY. PEOPLE COME AND GO A LOT. THERE ARE LOCALS, BUT THERE ARE ALSO PEOPLE FROM ALL OVER THE COUNTRY.
BECAUSE OF THIS, LOTS OF PEOPLE ARE NEW TO TOWN - OR, AT LEAST, REMEMBER BEING NEW. THIS MAKES BEING A RECENT ARRIVAL SURPRISINGLY EASY.
SO, DO YOU LIVE HERE FULL-TIME?
HAVE YOU BEEN HERE LONG?
THE DEMOGRAPHIC ALLOWS FOR A SERIES OF FOOLPROOF CONVERSATION STARTERS.
WHAT BROUGHT YOU UP HERE?
EAGER ALISON
(Before long I would be rolling my eyes at these questions.)
PEOPLE WERE NICE TO US. AND WELCOMING.
I REALLY DON'T SEE WHAT'S WRONG WITH BRINGING CHIPS AND SALSA.
THERE'S THAT QUINOA DIS
THAT'S ALWA A HIT.
OR WHAT ABOUT A BEET SALAD?
WE'RE OUT OF PROPANE FOR THE BURNE THOUG
NO. WE DON'T EVEN HAVE A BOWL TO MAKE IT IN.
SCRATCH
SCRATCH
THOSE SPINACH PHYLLO THINGS ARE GOOD, BUT WE'D NEE AN OVEN FOR THAT...
OR WHAT ABOU
EVEN IF IT WAS ONLY FOR THE SUMMER, I DEARLY WANTED TO MAKE FRIENDS.

AS IT TURNED OUT THOUGH, MY INABILITY TO MAKE INTERESTING CONTRIBUTIONS TO POTLUCKS WASN'T THE MAIN OBSTACLE TO DEVELOPING NEW RELATIONSHIPS.
YOU LIKE FISHING, MAN?
LET'S GO TOMORROW,
I KNOW THIS GREAT SPOT.
YOUR GIRLFRIEND CAN COME OVER HERE.
HANG OUT WITH MY GIRLFRIEND
YOU GIRLS CAN, LIKE, DO LAUNDRY OR SOMETHING.
SURE, WE MET PEOPLE QUICKLY...
WE'VE BEEN LOOKING AT THIS PLACE ON FORREST DRIVE,
...BUT IT TOOK TIME TO FIND A CIRCLE WE REALLY CONNECTED WITH.
IT'S $ 425,000
IT'S MORE THAN WE WANTED TO PAY, BUT IT'S BIG ENOUGH THAT WE COULD RENT OUT A ROOM.
OH, YEAH, IF YOU CAN GENERATE
WE'RE HAPPY
THE MORTGAGE RATES RIGHT NOW
PROPERTY
AS IT IS, WE'RE PAYING $2,200 A MONTH
ONLY A HALF
OH- AND THAT'S TO SAY NOTHING
I LIVE IN A MINI-VAN.

STILL, WE PERSEVERED ON OUR FRIENDSHIP QUEST.
WHEN INVITATIONS CAME OUR WAY, WE TRIED TO ACCEPT. THUS, WE WENT CAMPING TWICE THAT JUNE.
CAMPING TRIP #1
SOLSTICE
YOU'RE PRETTY LOW IN THE WATER.
BEER
FOR SOLSTICE, WE PADDLED OUT TO MOSHER ISLAND.
LET'S PLAY "GUESS THE TIME."
2 AM?
4:30 AM?
3:25 AM?
SLAP
2:30 AM?
WE WATCHED IT NEVER GET DARK,
UNTIL WE COULDN'T KEEP OUR EYES OPEN ANY LONGER.
mummble grmmmble
SORRY
I FORGOT THE TENT POLES.

AND THAT WAS THE END OF IT. NO MORE CAMPING. CONSIDERING THAT OUR HOME WAS A SOCCER MOM VAN, THE THRILL OF SPENDING EVENINGS SITTING OUTSIDE GETTING EATEN ALIVE WAS LOST ON US. WE WOULD BOND IN OTHER WAYS.

IN A SHOW OF GOODWILL, WE EVEN PARTOOK IN COMMUNITY EVENTS WE WOULD NORMALLY HAVE SNUBBED.
WHY ARE ALL THE KIDS' FACES SMEERED WITH GREEN AND BROWN?
THE MILITARY ARE IN CHARGE OF FACE PAINTING.
IT'S CAMO
HAPPY CANADA DAY.
ONLY TO BE REMINDED WHY THESE THINGS WEREN'T OUR CUP OF TEA.
THEN THE MUSIC FESTIVAL ROLLED AROUND:
WE VOLUNTEERED
WHAT DO YOU MEAN 'THERE'S NO BEER LEFT'?
SORRY
BUT IT'S ONLY 3PM ON SATURDAY!
SORRY.
WHAT ABOUT THE REST OF THE DAY? AND ALL DAY TOMORROW?!
UNTEER
WE STILL HAVE THIS WEIRD BLUE SMIRNOFF DRINK.
WE DANCED BARE-FOOT IN THE SAND
THIS IS AWESOME!
BUT MY FEET ARE SO DIRTY!
AND WE DON'T HAVE RUNNING WATER.
AND I'LL BE TIRED AND DRUNK WHEN I GET HOME.
AND WE FOUND KINDRED SPIRITS
JUST PUT CLEAN SOCKS ON BEFORE YOU GO TO BED!
THAT'S WHAT I ALWAYS DO.
PROTECTS THE SHEETS.

FROM THAT POINT ON, YELLOWKNIFE IMPROVED A LOT

SOMEWHERE CHEAP FOR LUNCH?
HA HA

GOOD INTENTIONS

EXPLORING
DESPITE NOW HAVING FRIENDS, WE STILL SPENT A LOT OF TIME TOGETHER OCCUPYING OURSELVES IN INEXPENSIVE WAYS.
RIDING OUR BIKES AROUND AND EXPLORING WAS A WEEKEND FAVOURITE.
SO MUCH FOR THAT LAST FRONTIER FEELING.
WAL-MART
Fred Henne Territorial Park
A Fed bear is a DEAD BEAR
DO NOT FEED WILDLIFE
HUH.
Long Lak
Range Lake
WHAT A NEAT VIEW OF THE CITY.
HURRY UP AND TAKE YOUR PHOTO!
¡¡SLAP!
SLAP!
Frame Lake Trail
I'VE GOT BLACK FLIES STUCK TO MY TEETH!

GRUNT.
YOU'D HAVE THOUGHT WE'D BE IN BETTER SHAPE BY NOW.
Yellowknife Dump
SO MANY SEAGULS...
SO MANY PEOPLE...
SALVAGE AREA
YK DUMP
Jackfish Lake
Back Bay
Niven Lake
Our Vacant Lot
YK Bay
SEE!
Shopping Centre Office Tower
22c
IT'S ALWAYS SEVERAL DEGREES WARMER DOWN-TOWN THAN IN OLD TOWN.
HOW CAN YOU KEEP ARGUING WITH THIS?!
N'Dilo (Yellowknives Dene)
A TIPI MADE WITH A BLUE TARP!
AND WITH A PROPER DOOR!

YOU KNOW, IT'S THE PERSON IN THE BACK WHO STEERS.
JUST PICK A SIDE TO PADDLE ON AND THEN STICK TO IT
I WOULD
BUT YOU'RE STEERING CROOKED

THE WOODYARD
FOR ALL OUR EXPLORING, OLD TOWN REMAINED OUR FAVOURITE PLACE,
AND WITHIN OLD TOWN, THE WOODYARD WAS THE AREA WE CAME TO FEEL MOST PASSIONATELY ABOUT.
THOUGH WE HAD HEARD ABOUT IT SOON AFTER GETTING TO TOWN, IT TOOK US A WHILE TO ACTUALLY FIND THE PLACE.
D'YOU THINK IT'S THERE?
DUNNO.
MOSTLY BECAUSE IT'S HARD TO NOTICE FROM THE ROAD,
I'M SURE THEY DON'T REALLY MEAN IT IN A HOSTILE WAY...
...RIGHT?
BUT ALSO BECAUSE IF YOU DO VENTURE CLOSER, IT'S EASY TO GET SCARED OFF BY THE BIG SIGN.
EINAR BROTEN
HISTORICAL AREA
Enter At Your Own Ris
Caretakers :

LUCKY FOR US, WE NOW HAD AN INSIDE CONTACT. SOMEONE TO TAKE US PAST THE SIGN. ONE OF OUR NEW FRIENDS WAS A SHACK DWELLER.
MAX LIVED IN THE WOODYARD.
OH MY GOD.
YOU LIVE HERE?

EINAR BROTEN
HISTORICAL AREA
YUP.
I RENT THAT WHITE SHACK.

AND SO, TO MY DELIGHT, MAX TOOK ME AROUND THE WOODYARD.

SO THIS IS OUR COMMUNITY COMPOST.

THE DOGS QUITE LIKE IT.

FRESH COMPOST
NO WOOD PLEASE

I WAS TREATED TO AN INSIDER'S TOUR OF THE HIGHLIGHTS.

WE GET WATER FROM THIS SINK IN THE SUMMER

IT'S GREAT.

THE BIG ONE IS KENZIE, HE'S SEBASTIEN'S DOG.

AND THIS IS MY PLACE!

I'LL SHOW YOU INSIDE LATER.

THE LITTLE ONES ARE GOOGLE AND GIZMO,

I'M NOT SURE WHICH ONE'S WHICH

THEY BELONG TO THE LANDLORDS,

TO MY LANDLORDS, I SHOULD SAY. DIFFERENT SHACKS HAVE DIFFERENT OWNERS.

THAT'S A DRAGON MOSAIC MURAL

JEN MADE IT WHEN SHE LIVED IN THAT SHACK.

NOW VICKY AND MARC LIVE THERE.

THIS IS SNOWKING'S HOUSE-BOAT
IN THE WINTER, THE SNOWCASTLE IS JUST OVER THERE.
THE LAKE IS FROZEN SOLID THEN, OF COURSE.
NOT SURE WHO THESE BIG TRUCKS BELONG TO.
THEY HAVEN'T MOVED IN YEARS.
THE BOMBARDIERS THOUGH, THEY GET USED.
THIS PLACE HERE IS RYAN'S
AND FRANKIE LIVES IN THAT SHACK WITH COUCHES ON THE ROOF.
IF YOU HAVE ISSUES WITH YOUR BIKE, YOU CAN ALWAYS ASK RYAN.

WE WERE BARELY A FIVE-MINUTE BIKE RIDE FROM DOWNTOWN, YET IT FELT A WORLD AWAY.
HEY BATISTE!
HEY MAX,
HEY ALISON
HI BATISTE!
I DIDN'T KNOW YOU LIVED DOWN HERE.
THIS IS AWESOME!
WHAT ARE YOU UP TO?
WHERE ARE YOU GOING?
OH
I'M JUST GOING TO PEE OVER THERE.
PEE?
OVER THERE?
YEAH.
YOU KNOW,
SOMETIMES, YOU JUST DON'T FEEL LIKE PEEING IN A BUCKET.
IN A BUCKET?
WELL, WE'LL LET YOU GET TO IT THEN.
WE'RE GOING TO HAVE A BEER AT MY PLACE.
JOIN US WHEN YOU'RE DONE.
A WORLD WHERE FLUSH TOILETS DIDN'T EXIST, AND WHERE PEOPLE CASUALLY MENTIONED URINATING IN PAILS.

I TOOK IT ALL IN WIDE-EYED.
I WANTED TO KNOW EVERYTHING ABOUT THIS WORLD.
SO, LIKE, WHAT DOES IT SAY ON YOUR DRIVER'S LICENSES?
MINE SAYS: SHACK NO.3, WOODYARD
I JUST INVENTED AN ADDRESS FOR MYSELF: * 1 RAGGED ASS ROAD.
PETER'S IS SILVER BULLET, I THINK.
MY FAVOURITE IS VICKY'S,
SHE HAD THEM WRITE "DRAGON SHACK" ON HER I.D.
IN THAT MOMENT, I WANTED MORE THAN ANYTHING FOR MY DRIVER'S LICENSE TO SAY 'DRAGON SHACK.'
I WANTED IT SO BAD.

Woodyard
THE MOSQUITO DANCE
SLAP
SLAP
SLAP
SLAP
SLAP

THE DEAL WITH THE WOODYARD

BOTH THE BORDERS AND THE IDENTITY OF THE WOODYARD HAVE SHIFTED OVER THE YEARS. INITIALLY THOUGH, IT WAS EXACTLY WHAT ITS NAME SUGGESTS: A LUMBER YARD.

SO, ORIGINALLY... the 1940s

(AN INFORMAL HISTORY OF AN INFORMAL AREA)

TWO NORWEGIANS, EINAR BROTEN AND HANS HANSEN, HAVE A BUSINESS SUPPLYING WOOD TO MOST OF THE TOWN AND TO THE TWO NEIGHBOURING GOLD MINES.

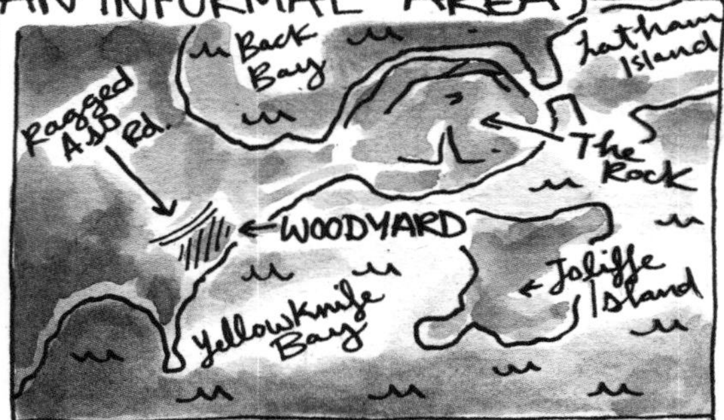

THEY OBTAIN A LEASE FOR A SMALL 100 FT x 200 FT PIECE OF UNTITLED LAND BETWEEN WHAT IS NOW RAGGED ASS RD AND THE SHORE OF YELLOWKNIFE BAY.

WHEN TAKING OVER THE LOT, EINAR BROTEN INITIALLY HAULS A FEW SKID SHACKS ONTO THE AREA FOR HIS EMPLOYEES TO LIVE IN.

OVER TIME, MORE AND MORE SHACKS POP UP. THE LEASE DOESN'T ALLOW FOR RESIDENCES – AND MANY OF THE NEW PEOPLE DON'T EVEN WORK IN THE WOODYARD...

... BUT THE ECLECTIC COMMUNITY GROWS IN HAPPY CHAOS IN A SEEMINGLY UNHINDERED WAY.

THE WOODYARD – CONTINUED

MID 1970s: EINAR BROTEN RETIRES AND SELLS MOST OF THE SHACKS TO A NEIGHBOURING FAMILY – STILL THE LANDLORDS TO THIS DAY. THE LAND, ON THE OTHER HAND, CANNOT BE SOLD. IN 1977, THE WOODYARD'S LEASE IS TERMINATED AND THE LAND IS RETURNED TO THE GOVERNMENT OF THE NWT – ALSO STILL CURRENTLY THE CASE.

OLD TOWN: THE TIMES A CHANGIN'

UP TO THE 1970s, THE WOODYARD WASN'T THE ONLY PART OF YELLOWKNIFE WHERE SHACKS AND GENERALLY UNSTRUCTURED LIVING WERE THE NORM. AT THAT TIME, OLD TOWN WAS STILL A HAVEN FOR TRAPPERS, COMMERCIAL FISHERMEN, BOOTLEGGERS, YOUNG COUNTER-CULTURE FOLK AND GROUCHY OLD TIMERS:

A PLACE WHERE THE CHAOTIC SPIRIT LIVED ON.

BY THE EARLY 1980s, THE TIMES WERE CHANGING. OLD TOWN, ESPECIALLY LATHAM ISLAND, WAS BECOMING A MORE **DESIRABLE** RESIDENTIAL NEIGHBOURHOOD. **NICER, BIGGER** HOUSES WERE GOING UP. AS WAS THE **COST** OF LAND AND REAL ESTATE.

MEANWHILE, THE **CITY ADMINISTRATION** WAS STARTING TO TAKE A KEENER INTEREST IN THE **DISARRAY** 'DOWN THE HILL'. AN EFFORT WAS MADE TO GET **ZONING** IN **ORDER**, AND TO **CRACK DOWN ON SQUATTING.**

PEOPLE **GOT ORGANIZED** AND **FOUGHT BACK.** THE 80s WERE TURBULENT, AS WERE THE 90s, AND THOUGH MANY **BATTLES** AGAINST THE CITY WERE WON, **MANY WERE LOST.**

YEARS OF CONFLICT TOOK THEIR TOLL – OF THE THIRTY ODD SHACKS STILL STANDING IN THE MID-80s ONLY A HANDFUL ARE STILL AROUND TODAY.

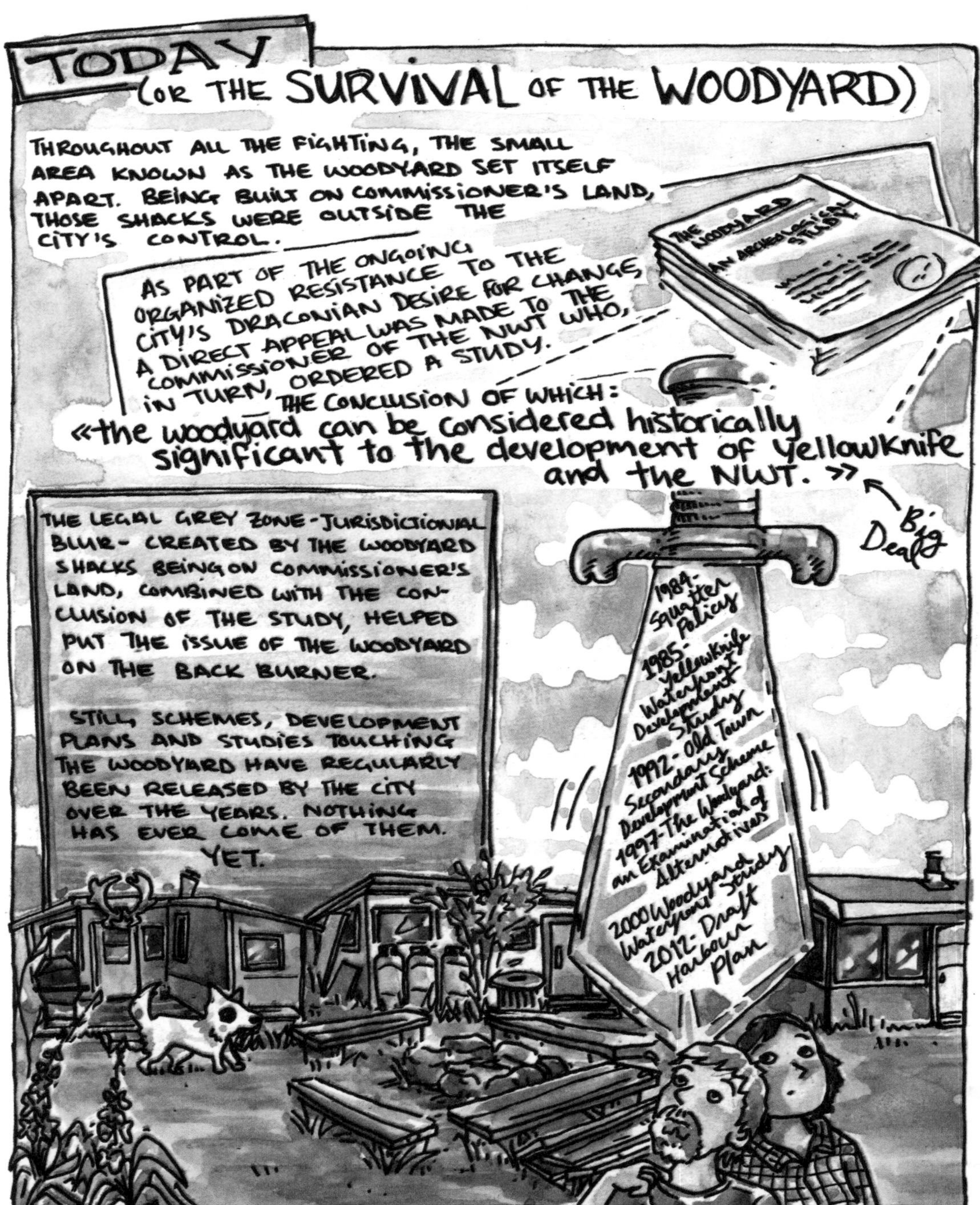
TODAY
(OR THE SURVIVAL OF THE WOODYARD)
THROUGHOUT ALL THE FIGHTING, THE SMALL AREA KNOWN AS THE WOODYARD SET ITSELF APART. BEING BUILT ON COMMISSIONER'S LAND, THOSE SHACKS WERE OUTSIDE THE CITY'S CONTROL.
AS PART OF THE ONGOING ORGANIZED RESISTANCE TO THE CITY'S DRACONIAN DESIRE FOR CHANGE, A DIRECT APPEAL WAS MADE TO THE COMMISSIONER OF THE NWT WHO, IN TURN, ORDERED A STUDY.
THE WOODYARD
AN ARCHEOLOGICAL STUDY
THE CONCLUSION OF WHICH:
«the woodyard can be considered historically significant to the development of yellowknife and the NWT.»
Big Deal
THE LEGAL GREY ZONE - JURISDICTIONAL BLUR - CREATED BY THE WOODYARD SHACKS BEING ON COMMISSIONER'S LAND, COMBINED WITH THE CONCLUSION OF THE STUDY, HELPED PUT THE ISSUE OF THE WOODYARD ON THE BACK BURNER.
STILL, SCHEMES, DEVELOPMENT PLANS AND STUDIES TOUCHING THE WOODYARD HAVE REGULARLY BEEN RELEASED BY THE CITY OVER THE YEARS. NOTHING HAS EVER COME OF THEM.
YET.
1984- Squatter Policy
1985- Yellowknife Waterfront Development Study
1992- Old Town Secondary Development Scheme
1997- The Woodyard: an Examination of Alternatives
2000 Woodyard Waterfront Study
2012- Draft Harbour Plan

NEIGHBOURS

FOR A TIME, WE WERE ALONE IN THE LOT

WE WERE FAIRLY INCONSPICUOUS,
OR SO WE LIKED TO THINK

AND THEN WE GOT COMPANY

THEY BLEW OUR COVER.

MR & MRS GERBRANDT WERE UP FROM GRANDE PRAIRIE. THEY WERE IN YELLOWKNIFE TO HELP THEIR SON DON BUILD HIS FIRST HOUSE. WELL, MR GERBRANDT WAS THERE TO WORK ON THE HOUSE. MRS GERBRANDT STAYED BACK AT THE RV AND PREPARED MEALS FOR HER HUSBAND AND SON.

HAVING THEM AROUND CHANGED THE DYNAMICS IN THE LOT. WE WERE NOW A SMALL- ALBEIT ODDLY MATCHED- COMMUNITY.

DO YOU THINK THEY'RE STILL AWAKE?
IT'S HARD TO SAY.
I REALLY NEED TO PEE, BUT I WOULDN'T WANT TO OFFEND MRS. GERBRANDT.
IF ONLY IT WASN'T BRIGHT OUT ALL THE TIME.

EVERY DAY, WHEN I GOT HOME FROM WORK, MRS GERBRANDT WOULD COME OUT FOR A CHAT. DILIGENTLY, WE WOULD DISCUSS THAT DAY'S WEATHER.

WE HAD QUICKLY LEARNED NOT TO STRAY FROM WEATHER. WHEN WE DID, IT GOT AWKWARD.

I WOULDN'T SAY WE BECAME FRIENDS, BUT WE WERE DEFINITELY NEIGHBOURLY.

COME AND COOK INSIDE!

AND WE WERE EVEN INVITED TO PARTAKE IN A FAMILY DINNER OR TWO,

JELLO SALAD AND ALL.

GOD BLESS THE...
GIVE THANKS FOR...
OUR LORD...
CHOMP CHOMP CHOMP
Don
his fiancée

AMEN
AMEN
AMEN
?
AMEN
PSSSST
PAAAT!
CHOMP CHOMP CHOMP

WE WERE SINFULLY LIVING OUT OF WEDLOCK IN A MINI-VAN.
MR & MRS GERBRANDT WERE GOD-FEARING GRANDPARENTS IN AN ENORMOUS RV.
IF THEY DISAPPROVED OF OUR PROMISCUOUS CHOICES, THEY NEVER SHOWED IT.
A POLICE OFFICER CAME BY THIS AFTERNOON.
I SEE THAT.
WE WERE DIFFERENT IN MANY WAYS, BUT JOINED BY OUR SLIGHTLY ILLEGAL LIVING SITUATION.
THIS TICKET SAYS THAT IF WE HAVEN'T MOVED BY 4:30, WE'LL GET TOWED.
DARN
WHAT TIME IS IT NOW?
5:15
MR. GERBRANDT TOOK CARE OF IT
TURNS OUT THE CITY DOESN'T HAVE JURISDICTION.
THE LOT WAS PRIVATE, AND MR. GERBRANDT HAD TRACKED DOWN THE OWNER.
NOW WE - ALL FOUR OF US - HAD PERMISSION TO BE THERE.

HITTING THE TOWN
OH!
I DIDN'T SEE YOU!
YOU SCARED ME!
DID YOU SEE ME CHECKING MYSELF OUT?
SO EM-BA-RAS-SING!
HEE HEE
IT'S 'CAUSE I'M ALL DONE UP TONIGHT.
ACTUALLY,
NORMALLY, LIKE, WHEN I'M AT HOME, I DRESS A BIT LIKE YOU.
LIKE, YOU KNOW, I JUST THROW ON WHATEVER.
WELL, I THINK IT'S COOL THAT YOU'RE OUT IN A BAR DRESSED LIKE THAT.
REALLY, WHAT MATTERS IS THAT YOU FEEL COMFORTABLE.
DON'T LET ANYONE TELL YOU OTHERWISE, GIRL.

AROUND THE SAME TIME AS THE AUTHORITIES WERE TAKING AN INTEREST IN OUR LIVING SITUATION, DIANE STARTED TO GET US INVOLVED IN THE HOUSE-SITTING BUSINESS.
HOUSESITTING
MY SCHEDULE'S ALREADY ALMOST FULLY BOOKED UNTIL SEPTEMBER,
BUT I KEEP GETTING NEW REQUESTS.
I CAN REFER THEM TO YOU GUYS, IF THAT'S SOMETHING YOU MIGHT BE INTERESTED IN.
IT'S NOT ROCKET SCIENCE: YOU GO OVER AND MEET THE HOMEOWNERS BEFORE THEY LEAVE TOWN AND THEY BRIEF YOU ON WHATEVER IS MOST IMPORTANT.
DIANE WAS LIKE OUR AGENT: SHE WOULD GIVE US NAMES, DATES AND PHONE NUMBERS.
WE WOULD TAKE IT FROM THERE.
I CAN'T BELIEVE WE'RE GOING TO STAY IN THE DINO-SAUR HOUSE!
YEAH...
BUT...
...DID DIANE TELL HIM WE WERE COMING?
DO WE JUST, LIKE, KNOCK AND INTRO-DUCE OUR-SELVES?
I GUESS...
WHAT'S THE GUY'S NAME AGAIN?
SHIT.
I FORGET.
WE FOUND IT SOMEWHAT AWKWARD.

PART OF OUR DISCOMFORT WAS THAT WE THOUGHT THE FAVOUR WAS MOSTLY ONE-SIDED.
AT THAT TIME, WE DIDN'T GRASP HOW HELPFUL OUR SERVICES WERE TO HOMEOWNERS.
RIDDLES HAS STARTED SEEING A SHRINK TO ADDRESS HIS UN-AC-CEP-TA-BLE BEHAVIOUR.
HE'S BEEN IMPROVING A LOT LATELY, SO IT'S IMPORTANT THAT YOU CONTINUE TO DEAL WITH THIS WHILE WE'RE GONE.
AS SOON AS HE STARTS BARKING, YOU MUST STOP HIM.
LET ME DEMONSTRATE.
WE TOOK IT ALL VERY SERIOUSLY
AND WE WERE INCREDIBLY GRATEFUL.
YOU NEED TO DOMINATE THE FENCE.
HE IS NOT THE BOSS OF THE FENCE
YOU ARE THE BOSS OF THE FENCE.
ENOU
RIDDLES
THIS IS MY FENC
GOT IT?
ENOUGH ABOUT HIM
I STILL HAVE TO SHOW YOU THE DAMN RABBIT.
COME
HE'S IN THE GARAGE
WE SMILED, NODDED AND TOOK IT ALL IN.

THE PRACTICE TANGERINE
AND THAT'S HOW YOU DRAIN THE CYST.
GOT IT?
ONCE A DAY SHOULD BE ENOUGH.
NOW FOR TOONA'S INSULIN SHOT.
LET'S GO OVER WHAT WE PRACTICED YESTERDAY.
HERE'S THE PRACTICE-TANGERINE.
YES.
YES.
GENTLY.
NOW SLOWLY BACK OUT.
AND THEN YOU RUB THE AREA A LITTLE.
SOOTHE HER SKIN.
RUB
RUB
RUB
A BIT LIKE WHEN YOU GET YOUR PUBES WAXED.
THE GIRL RUBS YOUR RAW SKIN.
AND THAT MAKES IT FEEL BETTER.
WELL, YOU KNOW HOW THAT FEELS.
HUM.
NO, ACTUALLY.
I DON'T.
OH.
HUM.
...

WE WERE HAPPY TO BE OUT OF THE VAN AND, BEING NEWCOMERS TO YELLOWKNIFE, IT WAS INTERESTING TO LIVE ALL OVER TOWN.

ON A LEASH, WE EXPLORED RESIDENTIAL NEIGHBOURHOODS.

IT WAS SUCH A CHANGE FROM WHAT WE HAD GROWN USED TO:
THE BIG EXPENSIVE HOUSES PARTICULARLY THREW US OFF.
WOW!
AND THE VIEW!
SO FANCY!
WHAT A BEAUTIFUL ROOM!
THE BED IS ENORMOUS!
...
...
WANT TO GO AND SLEEP IN THAT LITTLE GUEST BEDROOM DOWNSTAIRS?
BOTH BECAUSE WE FELT OUT OF PLACE,
AND BECAUSE THERE WAS SIMPLY TOO MUCH SPACE.
I CAN'T BELIEVE THEY DON'T HAVE A COLANDER.
THEY HAVE ONE.
I SAW IT EARLIER.
I CAN'T REMEMBER WHERE THOUGH.
ARG.
THIS IS CRAZY.
I'M STARVING.
THIS SHOULDN'T BE SO COMPLICATED.
HAVE YOU SEEN A CUTTING BOARD?

MOSTLY THOUGH, HOUSESITTING WAS MUCH OF WHAT YOU'D EXPECT:

A SEQUENCE OF FIRST-WORLD PROBLEMS FROM WHICH WE DREW CONCLUSIONS

SUCH AS:

HUH

WHO KNEW THERE WAS A DISHWASHER HERE...

EW! EW! EW!

Furry dishes

AND WHY DIDN'T THEY RUN IT BEFORE THEY LEFT?

NOTHING GOOD COMES OF A DISHWASHER FULL OF DIRTY DISHES LEFT UNNOTICED.

PAT! PAAAAT

FRONT-LOADING WASHING MACHINES ARE NOT INFALLIBLE.

FOR CRYING OUT LOUD
I HAVE THE HOUSESITTER NOTES HERE.
SUPPOSED TO BE RELAXING
HOW DOES THIS EVEN
LET'S TRY AGAIN.
"FIRST, ON THE TOSHIBA REMOTE PRESS ON THE

INSTRUCTIONS ON HOW TO USE REMOTES ARE INVARIABLY CONVOLUTED.

I CAN'T FIGURE IT OUT EITHER.
SORRY I MADE FUN OF YOU.
NO SHOWERS FOR US THIS WEEK.

SYSTEMS ARE NOT AS SIMPLE, OBVIOUS AND UNIVERSAL AS ONE WOULD THINK.

2 A SERIES OF SMALL LESSONS LEARNED ON PETCARE

AMONGST WHICH:

?

Formerly banana bread

THAT NO MATTER HOW SMALL THE DOG, THE COUNTER IS NEVER OUT OF REACH.

THAT GIVING A COCKER SPANIEL EARDROPS IS A TWO-PERSON JOB.

unfazed and unharmed

THAT TYING THE DOG UP IS NOT A SAFE WAY OF KEEPING IT FROM JUMPING THE FENCE.

? ?

HUMP HUMP HUMP

THAT THERE ARE TIMES WHEN IT'S IMPORTANT TO SHUT THE DOOR.

THIS IS CRAZY.
IT'S LIKE THE KEY JUST STOPPED WORKING.
... I HATE TO SAY THIS, BUT...
... I THINK WE MAY BE AT THE WRONG HOUSE...

POLYAMORY
ZZZZ
ZZZZZ
Z
ZZZ
ZZZZZ
ZZZ
HUM-HUM
ZZZZZ
ZZ
ZZZ
VERY CUTE.
BUT WHERE AM I SUPPOSED TO SLEEP?

I NEVER STOPPED BEING GRATEFUL FOR HAVING SOMEWHERE DRY AND BUGLESS TO STAY, BUT I DID GROW WEARY OF ALL THE PACKING AND HOUSE-CLEANING.

THIS IS THE FOURTH TIME WE'VE HAD TO MOVE IN TEN DAYS.

I CAN'T TAKE THIS ANYMORE.

HEH HEH HEH

CHECK THIS OUT!

WHEN I FLICK THIS LAMP SWITCH, THE FAX MACHINE AUTOMATICALLY TURNS ITSELF ON.

SIIIiiiiigh

ON

OFF

ON

OFF

HEH HEH

STILL, WE TRIED TO FIND PLEASURE IN THE SMALL THINGS.

OR, IF NOT PLEASURE, AT LEAST MILD ENTERTAINMENT.

DID YOU KNOW THAT IF YOU BLEW AIR INTO MY VAGINA, I COULD SUFFER A FATAL EMBOLISM?

SIIIiiiiiGH

YOU'VE GOT TO STOP READING THAT CRAZY OLD BOOK

PUT IT BACK WHERE YOU FOUND IT.

DARE I EVEN ASK?
WE PERSEVERED
I JUST GOT HOME.
IT REEKS OF CAT PEE REAL BAD.
HELP ME FIND WHERE THE SMELL IS COMING FROM.
SNIFF
SNIFF
SNIFF

SIGH.
CHRYSLER
Jeep

A REBEL AFTER MY OWN HEART
YOU'RE DRESSED?
YOU'RE GOING OUT?
IT'S AFTER 11 ...
... AND YOU HAVE A KNIFE?!?
I'M GOING TO BIKE OVER TO THE GREEN-STONE BUILDING.
I NOTICED THEY HAVE RHUBARB AS PART OF THEIR LANDSCAPING.
I WANT TO STEAL SOME,
MAKE A CRISP FOR DESSERT TOMORROW.

1 STALK, 2 STALKS, 3 STALKS
MMMMMMM
CRISP.

A REBEL AFTER MY OWN HEART

1 STALK,
2 STALKS,
3 STALKS
MMMMMMM
CRISP.
Canada

HONEY BUCKETS
MORE THAN GETTING TO STAY IN FANCY HOUSES THOUGH, IT WAS THE CHANCE TO SPEND TIME IN AN OLD TOWN SHACK THAT WE HOPED FOR.
YOU GUYS ARE DIANE'S FRIENDS WHO HOUSESIT, RIGHT?
Back living in the van between housesitting gigs
ARE YOU AVAILABLE THIS WEEKEND?
WHEN THE OPPORTUNITY CAME UP, WE WERE THRILLED.
Plastic Virgin Mary figurine
I GUESS IT MUST BE THIS ONE
JUST OFF RAGGED ASS ROAD.
Gold coloured boxing gloves
AND HE SAID THERE WERE PLANES ON IT.
IT WASN'T THE WOODYARD, BUT STILL...
...THERE'S A VIRGIN MARY IN BOXING GLOVES.

THE HONEY BUCKET IS IN HERE.
THEY COLLECT THEM ON WEDNESDAY. NEW BAGS ARE UNDER THE COUNTER-SAME AS THE TIE-WRAPS.
I'M NOT GONE LONG THOUGH, SO YOU SHOULD BE FINE.
YOU GUYS HAVE STAYED IN PLACES WITH HONEY BUCKETS BEFORE, RIGHT?
...
HUM.
YOU KNOW WHAT- DON'T WORRY ABOUT IT. I'LL TAKE CARE OF IT WHEN I GET BACK.
THIS WAS THE REAL DEAL. THIS WAS WHAT WE PICTURED TO BE THE QUINTESSENTIAL YELLOWKNIFE EXPERIENCE.
4
SO MUCH SO THAT WE EVEN TOOK PHOTOS OF OURSELVES LIVIN' THE SHACK LIFE.

THE DEAL WITH HONEY BUCKETS
YELLOWKNIFE'S OLD TOWN IS BUILT ON ROCK*
* SEE "The Deal with Trucked Water"
BECAUSE OF THIS, YOU CAN'T DIG A BIG DEEP HOLE
GN.
UNSUCCESSFUL
CANADIAN SHIELD
THAT RULES OUT OUTHOUSES AS WE PICTURE THEM DOWN SOUTH.
SO WHADDYA DO IF YOU DON'T HAVE PLUMBING BUT YOU CAN'T DIG A HOLE?
YOU USE A HONEY BUCKET!

A PRACTICAL GUIDE TO USING A HONEY BUCKET IN YOUR HOME
(The 2010 and after version)
1. GO TO THE STORE AND BUY A PACK OF BAGS*
NOTE: KIT CONVENIENTLY INCLUDES ZIP TIES.
PRICE FOR 10: $11.99
HONEYBAGS
FRUIT AND VEG SECTION
*Before 2010, the City supplied them
2. PUT THE BAG IN A STANDARD SIZED BUCKET.
Garbage Bag Style:
BAG
BUCKET
19.5 in.
3. FOR CONVENIENCE, IT IS BEST TO CONSTRUCT A USER-FRIENDLY SEATING OPTION.
"Store-bought toilet seat
Wooden box/bench structure
Honey bucket
When visiting, inquire into the household's toilet etiquette
4. SIT DOWN AND USE AS YOU WOULD A REGULAR TOILET
OR NOT
VARIATIONS ON THE THEME:
•PUT TOILET PAPER IN THE BUCKET
•DON'T PUT TOILET PAPER IN THE BUCKET.
•ONLY DO #2 IN THE HONEY BUCKET, PEE PEE IN SOME OTHER CONTAINER.
•ADD SAWDUST OR PEAT MOSS WHEN YOU ARE DONE
•ADD SAWDUST OR PEAT MOSS ONLY IF YOU DID #2.
etc.

5. WHEN DEEMED FULL, SECURELY TIE BAG SHUT WITH PROVIDED ZIP TIE.
Zip tie
Leave in bucket while tying
Some tips:
• For all subsequent transportation, leave in bucket whenever possible to avoid unfortunate accidents.
• In the wintertime, bags sometimes freeze to the bucket. Do not yank too hard when trying to unstick.
• Don't be afraid to let the bucket get quite full.
• Don't let the honey bucket get too full.
6. DISPOSE OF BAGS IN DESIGNATED AREAS.
Before 2010: PUT OUT IN COMMUNAL COLLECTION AREA FOR CITY TO REMOVE WEEKLY.
Since 2010: BRING TO DUMP YOURSELF AND THROW IN THE DESIGNATED DUMPSTER.
EEK!
Animal Waste & Honey Bags
If you are me, jump back after tossing, just in case.

BUT HE SAID TO LEAVE IT.
THAT HE'D TAKE CARE OF IT WHEN HE GOT HOME
OH, COME ON
WE CAN'T JUST LEAVE HIM A BAG FULL OF OUR POOP.

LATE-SUMMER LOVIN'
THE SUMMER WAS FLYING BY.
AS IS GENERALLY THE CASE, TIME PASSES FASTER WHEN YOU'RE HAVING A GOOD TIME. AND THAT, WE WERE.
THERE WERE PARTIES AND JAMS
AS WELL AS CASUAL AND COMPANIONABLE HANGOUTS
AND THERE I THOUGHT IT WAS SOMETHING PERSONAL,
AND THEN I REALIZED IT WAS BECAUSE I HAVE A VAGINA!
IT WASN'T PERSONAL. IT WASN'T AGAINST YOU. IT WAS AGAINST HALF THE PLANET!
AND, OF COURSE, THERE WERE SLIGHTLY INEBRIATED RANTS ABOUT PATRIARCHY, MYSOGINY, COLONIALISM, RACISM AND THE ALL-AROUND DISAPPOINTING STATE OF THE WORLD.
WE NOW HAD A LIFE IN YELLOWKNIFE. AS WITH ANYWHERE ELSE, IT'S THE PEOPLE YOU MEET WHO MAKE A PLACE.

I DON'T KNOW IF THERE WAS A PRECISE MOMENT WHEN WE OFFICIALLY FELL IN LOVE WITH YELLOWKNIFE,
BUT BY MID-AUGUST, WE KNEW THAT THIS WAS HOME.
SHE SAID THEIR SPARE CANOE IS THE BLUE ONE.
TO JUST GRAB IT.
THAT BLUE ONE?
OR THAT BLUE ONE?
ARG.
WE'RE SO LATE.
TAKE IT EASY.
IT'LL ONLY TAKE 5 MINUTES TO PADDLE OVER.
GREAT
THEN WE'LL ONLY BE 33 MINUTES LATE.

AND HERE'S THE SOUP.
BE CAREFUL
IT SLOSHES AROUND A LOT.
SOUP EH?'
WHY THE HECK ARE WE BRINGING SOUP?
WHAT WAS WRONG WITH SOMETHING SOLID AND STABLE LIKE BREAD AND CHEESE?
IT ALL JUST FELT SO RIGHT.

HOUSEBOAT PASTA
ARE YOU OKAY WITH ME COOKING THE PASTA IN WATER FROM THE LAKE?
RRRRRR
THAT'S WHAT I ALWAYS DO.
RRRRRRR
THE WATER'S REALLY PURE.
RRRRRRR
RRRRRRRRR
RRRRRRR
R-RRRRR
RRR-RRRR
RRRRRRR
RRRRRRRR
R-R-R
RRRRR

COMMITTING
AWESOME.

*NOTE FROM 2015 ▸ Élodie actually married the said date this past summer. Remember that folks: Dress down with jeans, then add flirty earrings.

NICE BEHIND.
EXCUSE-ME?
THE GIRL YOU'RE DRAWING, SHE HAS A BIG ROUND BOTTOM.
IT'S ME.
I NEVER NOTICED YOU ARE SO WELL ENDOWED.
EW.
ARE YOU EATING WHITE RICE WITH MUS-TARD FOR LUNCH?
YUP
I'D HAVE PREFERED KETCHUP, BUT MY DIET DOESN'T ALLOW IT.
THE NWT HAS THE HIGHEST CRIME RATE IN CANADA
YEAH. THAT'S A WELL-KNOWN STATISTIC.
OUR CRIME SEVERITY INDEX IS 314
WHAT DOES THAT MEAN?
DUNNO, BUT THE CANADIAN AVERAGE IS 68.

MOREOVER, BEING AT THE BOTTOM OF THE TOTEM POLE, ALL THE RANDOM UNASSIGNED TASKS SEEMED TO FALL TO ME.
ARE YOU STILL NOT DONE?
YOU'VE BEEN AT THIS FOR HOURS.
IT SHOULDN'T TAKE THIS LONG YOU KNOW.
I ASSEMBLED A SIMILAR ONE AT MY PLACE LAST WEEK AND IT ONLY TOOK ME AN HOUR.
YOU MUST BE DOING SOMETHING WRONG.
ENTERTAINING VISITING KIDS WAS A REGULAR OCCURENCE.
PLEASE!
PLEASE!
PLEASE!
OKAY.
BUT IT'S THE LAST TIME I TAKE IT OUT FOR YOU.
THE BIG EARRING!
I DID MY BEST.
SNIFF SNIFF
HUH.
IT SMELLS LIKE THE INSIDE OF MY VAGINA.

WHAT ARE YOU DRAWING?
SUMMER
OOOO. SUMMER. THAT'S NICE.
AND HOW DO YOU DRAW SUMMER?
A SUN.
SUN IS SUMMER
MOON IS WINTER.
WELL AREN'T YOU A TRUE NORTHERN GIRL.
IT WAS AN OKAY JOB, REALLY.

THE WILDCAT CAFE
ICE CREAM
IS IT NEW-YORK CHERRY-CHEESE CAKE?
NOPE.
GOOD GUESS THOUGH.

CULMINATION
WE KEPT ON MOVING
FROM HOUSE TO HOUSE, FROM PET TO PET
AND THEN WE GOT SOME GREAT NEWS
OH-MY-GOD THIS IS GOING TO BE SO COOL!
Going through a phase of eating store bought icing from the container as a snack.

IT WAS EARLY SEPTEMBER WHEN OUR FRIEND MAX GOT A JOB AT A MINING EXPLORATION CAMP.
Dragon Shack
Outdoor Sink
Fire Pit
Yaya
WHAT A CHANGE FROM THE BIG FANCY HOUSES WHERE WE'VE BEEN HOUSESITTING LATELY.
HE OFFERED US HIS SHACK FOR THE FIVE WEEKS HE WAS GOING TO BE GONE.
NO MORE DVDs AFTER DINNER.
NO MORE ENORMOUS TV.
NO MORE INTERNET
NO MORE SHOWERS IN THE MORNING
NO MORE FLUSH TOILET.
WE WERE THRILLED TO BITS.

LANDLORDS
SHED
Power
DRAGON SHACK
MAX'S SHACK
Honey bucket
odd indoor window
Hot plate
Water jug
Sink
Slop pail
stack of cushions
Mattress on the Floor
Bar fridge
Stools
Front door
disproportionate woodstove
Fake brick wall

IT WAS GREAT.
WE IMMEDIATELY FELT AT HOME.
KENZIE!
Yaya
Buttercup
Gizmo (or maybe Google)
C'MON IN!
Kenzie
Coldwell
Google (or maybe Gizmo)
I LOVED HAVING ALL THE NEIGHBOURS COME AND VISIT,
AND PAT LOVED THE RIDICULOUSLY BIG WOODSTOVE.
HEEEEEEY...
...PAAAA-AAAT...
ARE YOU COMING TO BED SOON?
NAH.
NOT JUST YET.
THIS IS AN AMAZING MARSHMALLOW FIRE.
GOTTA MAKE THE MOST OF IT.

MAX'S SHACK WAS A QUIRKY LITTLE PLACE.
ONE OF THE MOST MYSTERIOUS FEATURES WAS THE WINDOW THAT OVERLOOKED THE HONEY BUCKET.
HEY! DON'T LOOK!
I'M PEEING!
I'M NOT LOOKING, I'M CHOPPING VEGETABLES.
AND IF YOU WANT MORE PRIVACY, PLEASE FEEL FREE TO SHUT THE CURTAIN.
IT LET LIGHT THROUGH AND WAS LIKELY THE RESULT OF A DIY EXTENSION, BUT STILL
WEIRD.
SO DO YOU THINK IT'S TIME TO CHANGE THE BAG?
HMMMM.
IT'S NOT OVERFLOWING OR ANYTHING.
WHY DON'T YOU COME AND HAVE A LOOK?
...
I'M MAKING SUPPER.

ANOTHER QUIRK WAS THE FRONT DOOR THAT WOULDN'T STAY SHUT,
WE COULD INSTALL A LATCH?
OR MAYBE JUST A HOOK OF SOME KIND...
SNIF SNIF
WHAT'S WRONG WITH A BROOM HOLDING THE DOOR SHUT?
AS WAS THE LIMITED POWER SUPPLY.
STOP!
NEVER THE TOASTER AND
THE HOTPLATE AT THE SAME TIME!!!

IN SOME RESPECTS, WE HAD ADOPTED A FRONTIER STYLE OF LIVING. WITH THIS SUDDEN LACK OF BASIC AMENITIES, OUR DAY-TO-DAY ROUTINE WAS COMPLETELY DIFFERENT: EVEN THE MOST SIMPLE OF TASKS WAS NOW MORE COMPLICATED.

JUST BECAUSE WE DIDN'T HAVE RUNNING WATER, THAT DIDN'T MEAN OUR MODERN-DAY STRESSES VANISHED.

OH MAN.
I ONLY HAVE TEN DAYS LEFT BEFORE MY CONTRACT IS OVER.
TEN DAYS TO FINISH THIS REPORT.
IT'S LIKE I'M IN SCHOOL AGAIN AND THIS IS SOME BIG TERM PAPER
AAAARGH.
EXCEPT IN SCHOOL YOU WERE PAYING TO WRITE THE PAPERS
NOT THE OTHER WAY AROUND.
Work laptop
NEVER THE LESS, IN THE SHACK LIFE, EVERYTHING WAS CAST IN A SLIGHTLY MORE EXOTIC LIGHT.
WANNA TAKE A BREAK AND WASH MY BACK?

THIS DUALITY CARRIED OVER ONTO OUR INTERACTIONS WITH THE NEIGHBOURS
SO YEAH,
WE'VE GOT THIS GREAT SET-UP.
NO MORE SPONGE BATHS FOR US!
I'VE HUNG THIS POUCH - Y'KNOW, A SOLAR SHOWER LIKE YOU CAN BUY AT THE STORE - ABOVE A BIG RUBBERMAID CONTAINER.
IT'S LIKE THE REAL THING!
YOU SHOULD COME OVER AND SHOWER SOMETIME.
TRY IT OUT!
HEAT UP A COUPLE OF KETTLES OF WATER AND YOU'LL BE GOOD TO GO.
ALSO SIMULTANEOUSLY EXOTIC AND MUNDANE.
YAYA YAYA! YA-YA
YA-YA. YAYA
YA YA. YAAA YAAA
OH, COME ON...
MARC!
HOW OFTEN DO I HAVE TO TELL YOU?!
YAYA ISN'T ALLOWED OUT AFTER DINNER UNLESS SHE'S ON A LEASH!
...
YAYA! YA-YA YAAAA-
YAAAAA- YAAAAA
YAAAA YA-YA
YAYA YAYA
SHE'S A CAT.

OUR TIME IN THE SHACK COINCIDED WITH THE RETURN OF DARKNESS.
AAAAARG.
WHAT'S GOING ON?! IT'S THE MIDDLE OF THE NIGHT!
BEEP BEEP
WE SET THE ALARM FOR 2 AM.
WE'RE GOING TO GET UP TO SEE THE AURORA.
C'MON,
IT WAS YOUR IDEA.
WELL, IT WAS A STUPID IDEA!
AND WITH THE DARKNESS CAME NOT ONLY THE NORTHER LIGHTS,
BUT ALSO THE START OF BONFIRE SEASON.
MMMMMM
LET ME KISS YOU.
POOO-AH!
YOU TASTE AWFUL!
FRESHLY APPLIED BUG SPRAY.
IT WASN'T MEANT FOR YOU.
I SWEAR.

KNOCK 'N KNOCK
COME ON IN!
HEY.
I JUST THOUGHT I'D LET YOU KNOW THEY'RE TURNING THE WATER LINES OFF FOR THE WINTER ON MONDAY.
YOU PROBABLY WANT TO FILL ALL THE WATER JUGS YOU CAN-
HEY
ARE THOSE STACKS OF TRASHY MAGAZINES?!
I REALLY DIDN'T THINK YOU WERE THE TYPE...
KNOCK! KNOCK!
COME ON IN!
HEY-HEY, NEIGHBOURS!
WHAT'S UP?
WHAT THE HECK ARE YOU DOING, MARC?
HUH?
I'M BEING NEIGHBOURLY.
THE HEADLAMP?
THE FORK?
OH.
I'M BARBECUING STEAKS.
FORK'S TO FLIP 'EM.
LIGHT'S TO SEE WHAT I'M DOING.

WOW
IS IT THIS TIME OF YEAR ALREADY?
WHEN ARE THEY SWITCHING IT OFF?
TOMORROW, WE THINK.
WE'RE FILLING EVERY CONTAINER WE OWN
THA SUR RISI LY LAR E M JAR
THE TEA POT
SOME 2L BOTTLES WE FOUND IN THE RECYCLING BIN.
THE KETTLE
THAT BRITA JUG WE NEVER USE

CLINK
CLINK

JOLIFFE STOCK 2009
It's okay, it' alright, tonight i'll stay
trading in the wine for the moon- shine
I don't know if we're ever going to get there
the reflection in the water is always pink
THAT SEPTEMBER, WE LOVED YELLOWKNIFE.

BACK TO
JANUARY 2014
IS THAT YOUR DOG?
YEAH
THIS IS NINJA.
NINJA!
SHE LOOKS FROZEN, POOR LITTLE THING.
THAT'S WHAT SHE WANTS YOU TO THINK.
DON'T ENCOURAGE HER.
NINJA!
SUCK IT UP!
JUST SIT ON A PALLET.
OR GO PLAY WITH THE OTHER DOGS.
IF SHE WAS REALLY THAT COLD, SHE COULD JUST RUN ALONG HOME.
OH. DO YOU LIVE ON ONE OF THESE HOUSEBOATS?
NAH.
CLOSE ENOUGH THOUGH.
WE LIVE IN THE WOOD-YARD NOW.
IN THE DRAGON SHACK.

SO, FOR ALL YOUR TALK OF ONLY BEING HERE FOR THAT ONE SUMMER,
YOU NEVER DID LEAVE.
HUH?
OH.
NO.
WE LEFT ALRIGHT.
WE HIT THE ROAD AND TRAVELLED FOR THE BETTER PART OF A YEAR.
IT WAS AN EPIC JOURNEY.
BUT WE CAME BACK.
OF COURSE.

the End

ALISON A YELLOWKNIFE '09

Drawing in Max's Shack (Sept. 2009)

SOME UPDATES

The Van:

We bought the van for $650 in Quebec in May 2009. It seemed like it wouldn't last long, but it just kept running. Not only did it make it to Yellowknife, but it went from Yellowknife to Vancouver, to Santa Cruz, to Las Vegas, to Tennessee, back to Montreal and then back to Yellowknife. We never took it back to a mechanic after that fruitless visit in Alberta. It even kept going through a Yellowknife winter and, ironically, eventually met its demise through vandalism; a screwdriver through the gas tank finished it off.

The Vacant Lot:

A big plywood barricade was put up all around the lot by the following summer. It's high and unsightly, and we've always wondered if we and our fellow campers were to blame. Of course, far from being a deterrent to squatters, the fence has mostly made the area more private and hidden. Every season, it now sees a string of homeless folks set up makeshift camps behind the barricade.

The Woodyard Then:

My little history of the Woodyard is closely based on a section of Fran Hurcomb's book *Old Town, A Photographic Journey Through Yellowknife's Defining Neighbourhood.* Fran is a close friend and long time Old Towner and I thank her for bearing with my near plagarism.

The Woodyard Now:

In that same section, I explain that one reason the Woodyard has survived so long is because it's on Commissioner's Land and isn't under municipal jurisdiction. I mention the numerous development plans that could have affected the area over the years, but state that nothing much has come of them. In May of 2015, though, the land was transferred to the City of Yellowknife. Since then, we have seen surveyors doing their thing and planners with clipboards wandering through. At the time of writing these final notes, nothing tangible has changed, but we do worry. Oh, how we worry.

The Mosquitos:

I know this whole book makes Yellowknife sound like it's mosquito heaven – or human hell, depending on how you look at things. Really though, it's not generally that bad. 2009 was a bad year and, to make things worse, we were living outside. Come and visit and you won't get eaten alive. I promise.

Ninja the dog:

Ninja appears briefly on p.133. We adopted her in the fall of 2010 and she's been our faithful companion since.

Us:

As planned, we hit the road after that summer in Yellowknife. We travelled all over North America, spending the bulk of that fall working on an organic farm in California, and most of that winter making and selling jewellery in Mexico. We came back to Yellowknife in May of 2010 and, for all intents and purposes, we never left again. We housesat for another six months, went on to live in a houseboat, a crappy apartment and a couple of different shacks. Since May 2013 we've called the Dragon Shack home, and in March 2015, we had a baby, Riel, who now lives there with us.

NORTHWEST TERRITORIES
DRIVER'S LICENCE
NT
CAN
TERRITOIRES DU NORD-OUEST
PERMIS DE CONDUIRE
ALISON MC CREESH 15/08/1986
Name - Nom
1 MC CREESH
2 ALISON
5 DL No. - PC no.
3 Date of Birth - Date de naissance
1986/08/15
4b Date of Expiry - Date d'expiration
2018/08/15
9 Class - Classe
5
9a End - Endoss.
NONE
12 Conditions - Conditions
NONE
15 Sex - Sexe
F
16 Height - Taille
172 CM
17 Weight - Poids
68 KG
18 Eyes - Yeux
BLUE
19 Hair - Cheveux
BROWN
4a Date of issue - Date de délivrance
2013/05/29
8 Address - Adresse
DRAGON SHACK WOODYARD
YELLOWKNIFE, NT
X1A 1P1
4d Client No - Dossier no.
A McCreesh